"He's just a great artist, man, a great writer. He's one of my heroes, no doubt about it. How many great songs has he had? Sometimes I don't even remember the titles; I just remember the songs when I hear them."

— Abdul "Duke" Faker, Four Tops

"He's like an icon to everybody who writes songs. His songs last forever. The melodies are so infectious and they stay with you. You can walk away after a show and sing all his songs because they have that reminiscing, haunting thing about them."

— Lamont Dozier,
Hall of Fame Motown
songwriter

"When Neil Diamond sings, you know it's Neil Diamond. . . . You can play 'Sweet Caroline' anywhere in the country, and everyone's going to sing. That's something you can't take away. . . . Neil Diamond, he's still the man. As long as he can keep putting those shows on, he'll always be relevant."

— Darius Rucker,
Hootie & the Blowfish

"I got a chance to see Neil Diamond with Barbra Streisand. . . . Just the fact you've heard Neil Diamond years ago, growing up listening to your parents listening to Neil Diamond, to see him in person and he still had the same chops, it sounded like he didn't miss a beat. And what amazed me was the crowd he was performing for was a very cynical crowd because it was in L.A., and he came out and knocked their heads off."

— Jamie Foxx

"I must admit, to tell you the truth, in the early days, I wasn't the biggest fan. But I now am. I love him, I love him . . . you've got to look at what he's written; it's not just the stuff he sings. . . . That's the depth of Neil. I think he's fantastic. I nearly got his autograph."

— Paul McCartney

"He's one of the greatest of all time, as a songwriter and as a performer . . . as a person, he's one of the great people of all time. The subjects he chooses and the way he chooses to express himself is so unique. All of his songs, they're just a little off-center, and that makes them so interesting. They're saying all the things we need to say as songwriters, but he's found a wonderful way of doing it."

— Barry Manilow

"I love Neil Diamond. I've seen Neil Diamond a dozen times. The times I've seen him, it did everything for me that I need a concert to do. He's a great stylist of his own material. He's a great songwriter. He's got a great band. . . . In the E Street Band, some of our favorite songs to just screw on at sound check are what we consider bubblegum songs [and] I don't think anybody's written a better rock song than 'Cherry Cherry.' Basic rock. The hardest thing to do is write a three-minute rock song. Very few people do it better than Neil Diamond throughout the breadth of his career."

— Max Weinberg, drummer for Bruce Springsteen & the E Street Band and bandleader on The Tonight Show with Conan O'Brien

"He's an original, you know. He was such a romantic—still is. And he stands alone and sings his songs. He's great."

— Liza Minnelli

NEIL DIAMOND IS FOREVER

THE ILLUSTRATED STORY OF THE MAN AND HIS MUSIC

For Diamondheads everywhere,
especially Marlee Ruane, a devoted and discriminating fan who, since 1976,
has called me about every important development in Neil's career.

First published in 2009 by Voyageur Press, an imprint of MBI Publishing Company, 400 First Avenue North, Suite 300, Minneapolis, MN 55401 USA

MBI Publishing Company titles are also available at discounts in bulk quantity for industrial or sales-promotional use. For details write to Special Sales Manager at MBI Publishing Company, 400 First Avenue North, Suite 300, Minneapolis, MN 55401 USA

Library of Congress Cataloging-in-Publication Data
Bream, Jon.
  Neil Diamond is forever: the illustrated story of the man and his
    music / Jon Bream.
    p. cm.
  Includes index.
  ISBN 978-0-7603-3675-5 (hb w/ jkt)
  1. Diamond, Neil. 2. Singers—United States—Biography. I.
    Title.
ML420.D54B74 2009
782.42164092—dc22
[B]
                    2009007894

Front cover: Staples Center, Los Angeles, October 4, 2008. *© Kevin Estrada/Retna Ltd.*

Page 1: *Photo by CA/Redferns*

Page 3: Chicago Stadium, 1982. Neil asked photographer Cindy Shunko Jacobsma from stage if she was holding a camera or a telescope. Then he asked, "What color underwear am I wearing?" Cindy replied, "You aren't wearing any," which he repeated into the microphone for all 20,000 fans to hear. Then he winked straight down into her lens (which she captured), and in the next instant turned around and dared her with this pose. "I'm no fool," Cindy says. "Thank goodness for power winders." *Cindy Shunko Jacobsma*

Pages 6–7: Tickets. *Courtesy Peggy Mayers*

Page 9: *Photo by Michael Ochs Archives/Getty Images*

Page 11: *Photo by Waring Abbott/Michael Ochs Archives/Getty Images*

Page 12: Greek Theatre, Los Angeles, eight-show stand, September 13–20, 1976. *Photo by Michael Ochs Archives/ Getty Images*

Editors: Dennis Pernu and Amy Glaser
Design Manager: Katie Sonmor
Designer: Sarah Bennett
Cover Designer: Wendy R. Lutge

Printed in China

Contents

Introduction

Everybody's read one: a review deriding Neil Diamond as the "Frog King of Rock" or the cheesiest purveyor of pop on the planet. He is parodied on *Saturday Night Live*. The keepers of the Rock and Roll Hall of Fame haven't thought enough of Neil to even put his name on the ballot, let alone induct him.

He'd get my vote. I'm a believer in Neil Diamond. The naysayers can say what they want. That's okay. Neil fascinates me because A) he connects with his fans the way that my great rock heroes do with theirs and B) his life is the compelling story of a shy, quiet guy who overcame agonizing self-doubts and nagging insecurities to reign as the uncrowned king of pop for how many decades now?

For me, the audience is where it begins. There is a magical bond—a sense of comfort and awe—between Neil and Diamondheads. He connects with his crowd and thrills and satisfies them with marathon concerts just like rock gods Bruce Springsteen, Prince, and Neil Young have done for decades with their faithful. Like Young's Rusties, Boss believers, or even good ol' Deadheads, Diamondheads will travel from city to city, night after night, wearing Neil T-shirts new or old, carrying handmade signs and small cameras. So what if it's the same set list that he played the night before? It's NEIL! These fans will gush about his songs and charisma, his spirit and enthusiasm, his age-defying energy, and his derrière, if you know what I mean.

For more than thirty years, Neil, the enduring megastar, and I, the music critic in Middle America, have conversed about this connection. It's rare to have this kind of ongoing, long-term dialogue, especially one in which the same topic is revisited. It's even rarer for a pop figure to experience this kind of long-lived link with his audience that seems to grow stronger with every tour. Neil doesn't fully understand it, but he's not complaining.

In a 1986 chat, I pointed out that his adult audience behaves the way young people did when Elvis Presley

Performing at a music industry convention, Los Angeles, August 1976, the same year the author first interviewed Neil. *Photo by Sony BMG Music Entertainment/Getty Images*

was king or Bruce Springsteen was becoming the boss. I asked Neil, "Why do you cause this strange kind of fanaticism in *adults*?"

"I think they have good taste," he said over the phone. "You'll have to write 'he laughed when he said that.' He laughed . . . he said he laughed."

Okay, he didn't really laugh. He just said he laughed. He has a dry sense of humor. Very dry. And it seems even drier over the phone.

Take the time I asked him how much his sex appeal had to do with his popularity as a concert attraction: "If I had to make it on my sex appeal, I don't think I'd fill the Minneapolis arena three nights. I may only fill it one night." Ba-dum-ching!

We've had seven phone conversations since 1976. Whether I praised or panned his previous concert or album, he dutifully called and was always willing to talk about whatever subject I brought up. We've discussed everything from his songwriting and his self-doubts to his smoking (he quit in the late 1980s and, as a result, was able to add six or seven more songs to his shows) and that posterior that women think is so good ("I'm still working on it; that's why I have a trainer."). We've even talked about the Rock and Roll Hall of Fame (I'm a voter).

He speaks in an unmistakable brooding Brooklyn baritone. It's almost monotone, actually. In conversation, he's not the animated Man of 1,000 Gestures that he is onstage; but on the phone with me, he's always been unhurriedly thoughtful, with filler "uhs" and "ahs" punctuating the pauses. While he may answer questions with measured deliberateness, it sometimes seems as if he's not being forthcoming. He pauses as if he's contemplating some major revelation and then utters something simple and profoundly innocuous, vague, or elliptical—a bit like some of his lyrics.

Check out this exchange from our 1992 interview:

Q: Robbie Robertson [producer of Neil's 1976 *Beautiful Noise*] said you fill this musical vacuum between Elvis and Sinatra.

A: Yeah, I know Robbie said that. What do you think?

Q: It's really hard to explain. I saw Elvis in his last years and Frank two weeks ago, both certainly past their prime. But you seem as strong as ever even though you haven't had the big hit single or the multiplatinum album for years. Elvis and Frank would do one arena show and you're doing *three* shows. The parallel I pointed out on your last tour is that it's more like the Grateful Dead and the Beach Boys. You are these institutions with huge, dedicated followings, and you have these spiritual connections with your audience; it doesn't matter whether you have a new album or whether you

had a hit single on the radio three years ago or five years ago or last week, the connection is still there. There doesn't seem to be any other phenomenon like that in the history of popular music.

A: Well, I'm happy about it. I can't really explain it myself. I like to think my people have stayed loyal to me because of the music and because that's good. I like to think that's the bedrock foundation of the whole thing. Everything else is window dressing. Maybe I'm wrong. Maybe I'm naïve. But that's what I work on and that's what I think about. I have a relationship with my audience after all of these years. It's a special relationship. They know I'm never going to let them down. Not if I can help it, anyway. You go figure it out from that. I'm just going to enjoy it.

> **Y**ou understand this is one of the quintessential artists of our time, of the last one hundred years, someone we should laud and we should applaud for his innovations and for his musical abilities. Very few artists can be revered in their sixties and onward. He's definitely one of those people that is in the Hall of Fame of Hall of Fames.
>
> **—Brian McKnight**

That special relationship does sometimes extend beyond the stage. "I do read the letters once in a while," he told me. "I'll get them in a hotel or something will come into my office that one of the secretaries wants me to see. I will see the fans when I'm out touring. Sometimes they'll be in the hotel, sometimes they'll be outside of the venue if it's not too cold. There are fans that have been fans for years; so I know they're friends of mine and they're invited to all the shows when we come to their town. But realistically I don't have a lot of contact other than that. When I'm out touring, it's about resting, getting myself into shape, and doing the show. But I like to meet fans. It's neat. They're mostly very cuddly. They all want a hug. And I give out as many as I can. It's my form of safe sex."

Of course, the delivery of that punchline was as dry as a day-old bagel.

In all the interviews over the years, Neil has been strikingly polite (he once thanked me for working

Neil's triumphant turn at the Glastonbury Festival, Glastonbury, England, June 29, 2008. *Photo by Danny Martindale/WireImage*

After my first interview with him back in 1976, Neil asked me to send him a copy of the write-up for his files, and he gave me the address of his office on Melrose Avenue. Ten years into a stellar career and he's still keeping a scrapbook? During almost every interview, he's invited me to stop by and say "Hi" after his next show in St. Paul or Minneapolis. I never have because I'm usually busy up in the press box writing my review for the *Minneapolis Star Tribune*. A deadline beckons when you are a critic for a daily newspaper.

One time I did stop by before the show because Neil's publicist extraordinaire, Sherrie Levy, wanted to give me and my four-year-old son a tour of the bowels of Neil's revolving theater-in-the-round stage. After our tour, which enthralled my theater-loving son to no end (he couldn't believe all the electrical wires wrapped around a pole as the stage revolved in the same direction), we stopped by the catering room for a preshow snack. Who should walk in wearing a white terrycloth bathrobe? You guessed it. I almost didn't recognize him because—well, you know that line about the frog who dreamed of becoming a king? It looked as if he'd just come out of the shower and the nonchalant king's hair had been styled by a towel, not a comb.

There is a Yiddish word often used to describe Neil. It's *mensch*. His grandmother would have translated it as "nice Jewish boy who does everything his parents expect of him." But the dictionary defines it as a "decent, upright, mature, and responsible person." That's the way he's impressed me in our series of conversations over the past thirty-four years. That's the kind of guy he was in August 2008 when, after giving a subpar performance in Columbus, Ohio, due to laryngitis, he offered refunds the next day to eleven thousand concertgoers. But Rich Wiseman, in his well-researched 1987 book, *Neil Diamond: Solitary Star*, describes Neil as having the characteristics of both a *mensch* and a king. Although Wiseman didn't interview the singer, he conducted more than one hundred interviews over the course of three years with former Diamond associates, collaborators, and employees. He gives you the dirt and warts, the diva

on Sunday) and unfailingly gracious, even if I asked a question that might have made him uncomfortable. For instance, in the summer of 2008, I said, "You will be the oldest solo male performer to do an arena tour of this magnitude. Did you realize that?"

"Well, I didn't know that," the then-sixty-seven-year-old responded with a feigned chuckle. "I do know that I'm the oldest recording artist in the history of Billboard charts to have a No. 1 album, which I kind of halfway love the idea. Of course, it's nice to be No. 1 in anything, but I do like the idea. Oldest, youngest—it doesn't matter. I feel great. I'm singing very well. That's the main thing."

MusiCares Person of the Year tribute, Los Angeles, February 6, 2009. *Photo by Rick Diamond/WireImage*

and the rough Diamond, and discusses nearly every legal action, kerfuffle, and plan gone awry in the first two decades of Neil's career.

The book you're holding isn't about that kind of muckraking. This is about Neil Diamond's story in words and photos. He is indeed a solitary man, an obsessive workaholic who goes to the office every day to write, whether he has an idea or not, a famously wealthy and accomplished superstar who thinks he's only as good as the last song he wrote, a brooder wracked by agonizing self-doubt and nagging insecurities, a neurotic New Yorker who has gone through more therapy than bottles of red, red wine. Am I good enough? Should I have become a doctor? Will the audience still love me? Why has disappointment haunted all my dreams?

"It's not my nature to be happy," Neil told me in 1986. "Satisfaction, contentment—those are more like it. I'm happier as a person now, I'm happier with myself. I feel more at ease with myself. But I'm not happy with a capital H."

Neil sees himself as a simple man. Asked to give ten adjectives to describe what Neil Diamond is really like, he demurred. "It's much simpler than

ten—maybe three or four. What's he like? He's like what he was when he was seventeen except he's got a lot more responsibility; a lot more expected of him. But he will always be seventeen."

Diamond never envisioned this fabulous career in which he's sold more than 125 million albums and performed in front of millions of concertgoers, including 170,000 in just one show at Glastonbury, England, in 2008. Ever the self-doubter, he thinks luck has played a key role in his story. "I never planned to be a singer. I never planned to sell out three shows in Minneapolis," he told me. "I only hoped I could write songs one day and earn a living doing that because that was the thing I loved doing most. The rest of it seems like one giant accident. A little bit of talent and a tremendous amount of hard work and a lot of fun, also. But it was not planned out in any way, shape, or form. I was as shocked as anyone else could be. I was a very shy, quiet kid. I'm a quiet person. I'm not extroverted at all except when I hit the stage. Then this other person comes out."

—*Jon Bream*
Minneapolis–St. Paul, February 2009

Prelude: Everyone Goes, Everyone Knows

Q: Have you ever thought of doing a Las Vegas residency?

A: I like the idea of going to people's hometowns. I really do. I don't want to get stuck in a single place and have them come to me. I feel like it's one of my obligations as an artist to come to people's hometowns and play my music for them. That's one of the reasons I do it.

—Neil Diamond, 2008

Hot July night. Okay, maybe not "Brother Love" hot, but there is tent-revival-like electricity in the sold-out Xcel Energy Center filled with sixteen thousand Neil Diamond diehards.

It is the opening night of the pop icon's first North American tour in three years. A new album, a new tour, a renewed excitement. It's not just another new album, it's Neil's first No. 1 album ever. *Home Before Dark* sold 146,000 in its first week. Not bad for a guy who hasn't had a radio hit in more than two decades.

The seemingly ageless sixty-seven-year-old überstar already performed in Europe during the summer of 2008 and earned rave reviews, especially for playing in front of 170,000 at England's Glastonbury Festival in the prestigious "legends" slot. With several shows behind him, Diamond came to St. Paul, Minnesota, a day early for a rehearsal.

He doesn't treat opening night any differently than any other night. "It's not different, it's pretty much the same," he told me a few days earlier. "It's one guy supported by a wonderful band presenting music to an audience that, hopefully, is receptive and looking to have a good time."

He knows his audience. There's Marlee Ruane, 77, who has seen every Diamond concert in the Twin Cities since 1972. Michelle Stimpson, 39, is in the second row with her husband, Bill. They have tickets to the first four shows on the tour. Jim Novak, 35, is wearing his unofficial, custom-made Neil Diamond sweatband (featuring an unauthorized caricature of the icon) that's part of his uniform for a softball team lovingly dubbed the Neil Diamonds. His wife, Dawn, 40, handles marketing for the oldest and hippest head shop in Minneapolis, the Electric Fetus, but grew up listening to Neil's music. As a kid, Jim used to act out "America" while listening to *The Jazz Singer* soundtrack as he cleaned the house. Jim and Dawn introduced their parents to one another at—what else?—a Diamond concert seven years ago.

"It's a great audience," Diamond says of the Twin Cities, but he might say that about every audience. "They've always been very kind to me," he continues, sounding more humble than forlorn. "It's a great upper to kick the tour off here."

The house lights dim, and in an age-old concert ritual, the fans rise to their feet. The band is in place, and suddenly the man of the night appears at the back of the stage, backlit, guitar strapped over his shoulder. "I've been away from you too long," he bellows like a homecoming hero in the same arena where, a few weeks later, Barack Obama will hold a rally to celebrate clinching the Democratic Party nomination for President of the United States and where, a few weeks after that, John McCain will be nominated by the Republican Party.

I liked his work a long time ago. I saw him at Glastonbury [in 2008], and it was amazing . . . it was good music and thousands of people were singing along with him. I know how that feels. It feels very whoop-dee-doo. So he was in a whoop-dee-doo mood, which was sort of touching.

—Joan Baez

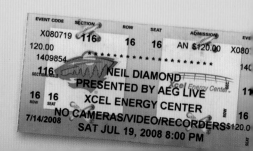

There's no form of exercise that will prepare you for two hours of singing on stage and performing for an audience. You can't do sit-ups and you can't lift weights or do Pilates or yoga because it's meaningless. There's nothing that can duplicate the required energy and spiritual, psychological, physical vibe that you have to put out. The only way to get yourself in shape is to actually do it. After you've done it a bit, you're ready to do it some more.

—Neil Diamond, 2005

In 2008, Diamond looks different, ready for a new campaign of his own. Trimmer, younger even. He's wearing a black sport jacket, not one of those familiar garish beaded shirts. So much for his long-held contention that he dresses loud to be seen. Underneath the coat is a black shirt with some tastefully understated embroidery on the front. The shirt is untucked, just like those fashionable college boys.

The Frog King turned Mr. Forever Young opens with "Holly Holy," a fittingly reverent celebration for a No. 1 album. In mid-song, he shouts a greeting: "Hello Saint. . . ." Oops. Something goes wrong. The mic? The sound system? Whatever it is, "Paul" is not heard, and that puts the brooder from Brooklyn in a foul mood.

More perfectionist than professional, the singer seems to be in a funk for much of the night. After "Love on the Rocks" and "Play Me," he declares, "Enough anguish, enough torment. It's time to dance." But "Cherry, Cherry" isn't as vibrant and dynamic as usual. He seems to be lacking concentration, and his voice is missing its usual oomph. He sounds brooding on the new "Don't Go There" and somber on "Solitary Man." "Forever in Blue Jeans" comes across as more meat-and-potatoes than the usual ham-and-cheese. But "Sweet Caroline" is the pick-me-up for the singer and the crowd. It sounds so good, so good, so good. "I'm a Believer" is all funked up with horns, and "Hell Yeah," from the 2005 release *12 Songs*, is his most passionate vocal, although it's a quiet song and an odd choice to end the main set.

However, Diamond knows how to crank it up for the encore with the clap-along "Cracklin' Rosie" and the celebrative "America," the ideal song of determination in this election year, just the way it became a rallying cry at Neil's post-9/11 shows. The Diamondheads are going wild. They know his exit is just part of the routine. "Brother Love's Traveling Salvation Show" is coming next, right? He's closed every show with that stir-it-up pop/gospel mashup for nearly four decades now.

The house lights go up. What? Opening night is over. There was no "Paul" at the beginning and no "Brother Love" at the end. ✦

Brooklyn Cowboy

1

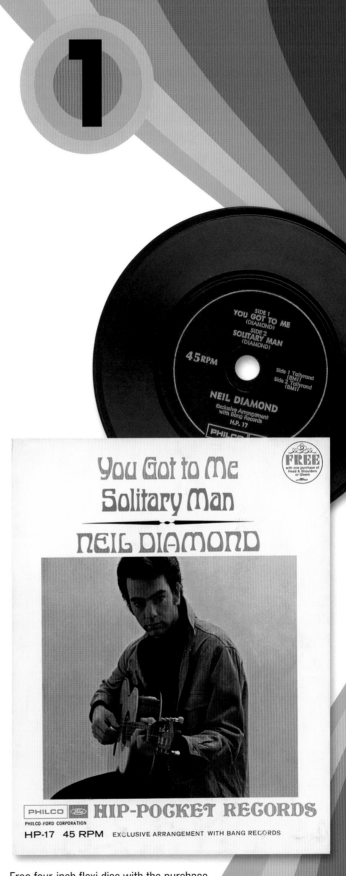

My father was an amateur theatrical buff. Let anyone announce they were putting on an amateur show anyplace and he'd drop his tape measure and run to offer his services.

—Neil Diamond, early press release

Neil Diamond. That's his real name. He toyed with using pseudonyms—Eice Cherry and Noah Kaminsky—when he was about to release his first album. Neil Leslie Diamond was born in Coney Island, New York, on January 24, 1941, to Rose and Akeeba (Kieve) Diamond.

Kieve's parents, Sadie and Abram, were from Poland; Rose's parents, Molly and Abraham Rappaport, were from Russia. Rose and Kieve's other child, Harvey, arrived on January 19, 1943. Kieve ran a stationery shop and then served in the army, which stationed the family in Cheyenne, Wyoming, in 1944.

"I think Cheyenne had a big influence on me," Neil Diamond told *Rolling Stone* in 1988. "That's where I got my love of cowboys. Because I always thought I was one after I came back from Cheyenne. A Brooklyn cowboy."

After four years out West, the Diamonds returned to Brooklyn, where Kieve operated a haberdashery for five years (maybe that's where Neil gets his sartorial flair) before opening Diamond's Dry Goods in 1953. Neil worked there, helping customers buy bras and underwear. Away from the shop, Kieve was an amateur performer of sorts, or maybe just a ham who could do a cheesy impression of Eartha Kitt. Maybe that's where Neil caught the showbiz bug.

Free four-inch flexi disc with the purchase of Head & Shoulders or Gleem!

NEIL DIAMOND
*Abraham Lincoln High School,
Brooklyn, N.Y. 1958*
Fencing Team; G.O. Councilman;
Choral; Sing; Class Nite.

Abraham Lincoln High School,
Brooklyn, 1958.

In his Brooklyn environment, Neil took a shine to all kinds of music that he was exposed to—from traditional Jewish sounds and nascent rock 'n' roll on the radio to R&B and the Latin jazz that his parents liked to dance to. The future pop star gave his first public musical performance at his bar mitzvah, but his pivotal music experience came the following year at Surprise Lake, a liberal Jewish camp about sixty miles from Manhattan where the friendly but crusading folk singer Pete Seeger performed for the young campers.

"Some of the kids played their songs for [Seeger] and they were all singing about causes, you know, whatever causes meant something to a fourteen-year-old," Diamond told *Rolling Stone*. "That was the first time I realized that my peers could write songs. And that I could do it, too, maybe, just for fun."

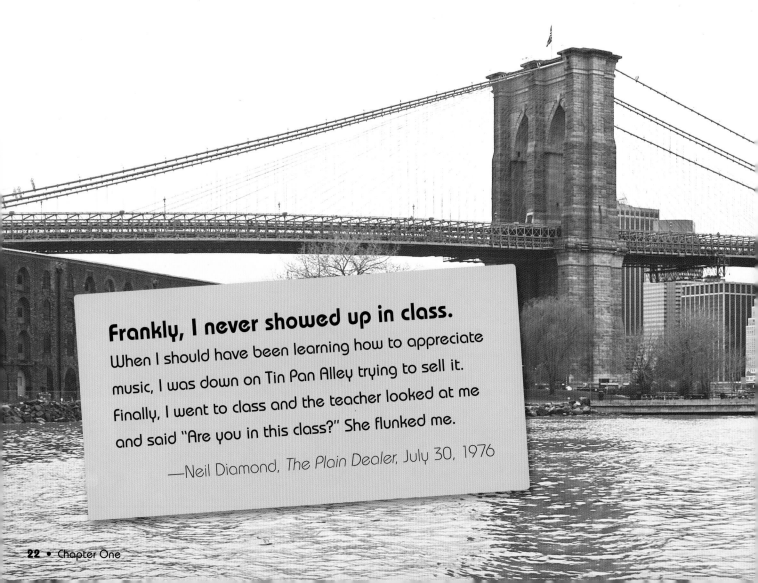

Frankly, I never showed up in class.
When I should have been learning how to appreciate music, I was down on Tin Pan Alley trying to sell it. Finally, I went to class and the teacher looked at me and said "Are you in this class?" She flunked me.

—Neil Diamond, *The Plain Dealer*, July 30, 1976

Neil got a secondhand guitar and learned how to play country and folk songs. He was intrigued by songwriting because "it was something no one in my family had done. It was unusual. It wasn't your everyday average kind of thing, and it was the first real interest I had shown in anything up until that point," he told *Rolling Stone*'s Ben Fong-Torres in 1976. It also provided an escape from his loneliness.

His songs and interviews make it sound as if Neil Diamond was born lonely. "I was a very shy, quiet kid," he told me in 1992. "Just an average, normal kid. Walked old ladies across the street, had friends, played basketball and stickball on the streets. Tried to be a good person."

He sang in the choir at Erasmus High School (along with Barbra Streisand, whom he didn't know at the time) and at Lincoln High, which he attended for his senior year. Two significant things happened to him at his new school: He joined the fencing team (making him "feel for the first time like a winner," he told *People* in 1979) and saw recent grad Neil Sedaka return to perform a pop song in the auditorium.

continued on page 26

> **The way I hold myself onstage and the way I stand,** maybe some of the movements I make are from things I learned as a fencer. . . . That's just the way I move. I couldn't get a choreographer to teach me how to dance. I just had to learn something that was just right and natural for me.
>
> —Neil Diamond, 1992

DJ promo copy of "You Are My
Love at Last" b/w "What Will
I Do," with Jack Packer as
"Neil & Jack."
Courtesy Bill & Jeff Collins

"You Are My Love at Last"
b/w "What Will I Do," with
Jack Packer as "Neil & Jack."
Courtesy Ralph Bukofzer

DJ promo copy of "At Night"
b/w "Clown Town."
Courtesy Bill & Jeff Collins

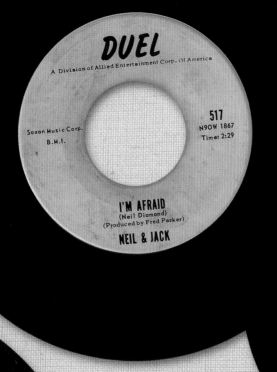

DJ promo copy of "I'm Afraid" b/w "Till You've Tried Love," with Jack Packer as "Neil & Jack."
Courtesy Bill & Jeff Collins

"At Night" b/w "Clown Town."
Courtesy Bill & Jeff Collins

> ## Bob Dylan
> made it possible for the composer to be also the singer. . . . I don't think I'd be here if it wasn't for Bob Dylan. No. I'd be in another business. I couldn't make it just as a songwriter. I'd been hired and fired from most of the major publishing companies in New York. They felt I had talent but they didn't know what to do with it.
>
> —Neil Diamond

continued from page 23

Inspired, the younger Neil got together with a new friend, Jack Packer, and they began performing as a duo at dinner dances. They continued performing while in college, releasing two singles—the Everly Brothers–influenced "What Will I Do" in 1960, followed by "I'm Afraid." While Neil and Jack were working as waiters in the Catskills resort area the summer before their freshman year of college, Neil met Jay Posner, a nice Jewish girl from Long Island who was headed to Hofstra University to study to become a teacher. She also would become not only the inspiration for his first pop composition (the doo-wop-infused "Hear Them Bells") but, eventually, Mrs. Neil Diamond.

Fencing landed Diamond a scholarship at New York University, where he enrolled as a pre-med student majoring in biology. His childhood dream was to become a doctor. In fact, when I asked him in 1992 if he could change anything in his life, he said, "I probably would have gone to medical school and become a brilliant research scientist and have cured cancer and AIDS, muscular dystrophy, and you name it. That's what I wanted to do when I was a kid. That's why I studied medicine, that's why I was a star science student. If this darn songwriting thing hadn't come up, I would have been a doctor now."

But that songwriting itch pulled him away from dissecting frogs and working on organic chemistry formulas. (School records show that

Early *Cash Box* ad.

MY SINCEREST THANKS, DEEJAYS, For Voting Me...

#1 MOST PROMISING UP AND COMING MALE VOCALIST! AND #3 MOST PROGRAMMED MALE VOCALIST!

NEIL DIAMOND

Exclusively on BANG RECORDS

CURRENT ALBUM: "THE FEEL OF NEIL DIAMOND"

FREDANA MANAGEMENT
FRED WEINTRAUB — BILLY FIELDS
180 THOMPSON ST., NEW YORK, N.Y.
(212) GR 5-7754

SPECIAL THANKS TO MY PRODUCERS
JEFF BARRY & ELLIE GREENWICH

PUBLICITY
JOE CAL CAGNO
BOX 96
ROCKVILLE CENTRE, N.Y.
(516) 536-7186

NEIL DIAMOND

Fields — Weintraub, Inc
211 East 51st ST.
New York, N. Y. (212) 355—1711

Early press photo.

Early recording session, circa 1963. *Photo by Michael Ochs Archives/ Getty Images*

Brill Building, 1619 Broadway, New York City. *Photo by Michael Ochs Archives/Getty Images*

In the early days

when Neil was peddling his songs in Tin Pan Alley, he allotted himself 35 cents a day for a meal: a 23-cent Hoagie, a Coke, and a two-cent piece of candy from Woolworth's.

—*Rocky Mountain News,*
   September 19, 1976

he switched to the school of commerce for a while, according to Rich Wiseman's *Solitary Star*.) He wrote lyrics during lectures and then cut classes to head uptown to Tin Pan Alley to pitch songs. "I never really chose songwriting. It just absorbed me and became more and more important in my life as the years passed," he said in the 1976 *Rolling Stone* interview. "I suppose if I were able to earn a living through fencing, I might have chosen that, because that also had its way to vent the emotion side of me."

After looking up "music publishers" in the Yellow Pages, the aspiring tunesmith landed a songwriting contract at Sunbeam Music for $50 a week and left singing partner Jack Packer and NYU. After Diamond's sixteen-week contract expired without any hits, he took the next step: as a recording artist. His first go-round with Columbia Records was short-lived. At his debut performance, the graceful fencer tripped over a wire onstage and fell on his face. The label let him go after just one single, 1962's "At Night." "That [song] was me trying to be Neil Sedaka and not even coming close," Diamond wrote on the liner notes to his 1996 boxed set, *In My Lifetime*.

So it was back to songwriting for the newly married college dropout. While his wife taught school and gave birth to two daughters, Diamond spent the next few years bouncing from one publisher to another in the Manhattan pop hit–making head-quarters known as the Brill Building. He became more and more introverted, but the lack of success provided some valuable lessons. That experience "taught me a great deal about people, it taught me a great deal about songwriting, it taught me a great

deal about survival," he told me in 1976. "It was really a very exciting time despite the failure for that period of time. Because it was all new and there was nothing really to live up to. Every day was new. There was a great deal to be learned. There were friends made, camaraderie established. It was a very exciting time. Especially during that period, music was going through tremendous changes, the country was going through tremendous changes, and I was going through enormous changes."

In the mid-1960s, he rented a storage room for $35 a month above Birdland, the famous Manhattan jazz club. It served as his songwriting office, equipped with an upright piano and a pay phone. To sing on a demonstration—demo—of one of his songs, he called the Demo Queen, Ellie Greenwich. She also happened to be partners with her husband, Jeff Barry, in a hot songwriting team, having scored hits with the Dixie Cups ("Chapel of Love"), Ronettes ("Da Doo Ron Ron"), and Shangri-Las ("Leader of the Pack"). The established pros hit it off with Diamond, formed a publishing company with him (he got $150 a week advance against future royalties), and agreed to produce Neil Diamond as a recording artist.

Writing for himself for a change, he crafted "Solitary Man," "Cherry, Cherry," and "I Got the Feelin' (Oh No No)." Barry took Diamond to Atlantic Records, where hit producer/vice president Jerry Wexler signed him. But Wexler's specialty was R&B (Ray Charles, Wilson Pickett), so he handed Diamond off to former staff producer Bert Berns, who was just starting an Atlantic-affiliated label, Bang Records. ✦

The songs I write are an extension of my personality. It would be only natural for me to want to record them.

—Neil Diamond, *Teen*, May 1967

Neil Diamond, Ellie Greenwich, Bert Berns, and Jeff Barry, circa 1965. *Photo by Waring Abbott/Michael Ochs Archives/Getty Images*

Competition For Diamond

NEW YORK — Neil Diamond of "Solitary Man" fame has been signed by Associated Booking Corporation, winner of the heated competition surrounding Diamond.

The agency competition for Neil had been building up since his smash "Solitary Man" and came to such a head when "Cherry, Cherry" was released that Diamond found it necessary to "duck out of sight for a week" while his attorneys went through the negotiation hassle.

Associated has high hopes for Neil. Says Sol Saffian, who will handle Diamond at Associated: "We expect Neil Diamond to become an artist of major importance. He has proven himself as a song writer and recording artist of consistant quality but even more exciting is the fact that as a performer in a business of look-alike — soundalike acts he comes across as an individual, one who is able to develop a very personal rapport with his audience. We are very pleased to have this fresh new talent with us."

Although Neil has played with roughly 40 groups, he says he really got started about two years ago. "Before it was just to make a buck. I used to write poems and things and then I started putting them to music and I liked what I was able to do. I wrote for other people — Sonny & Cher, Bobby Vinton, Andy Williams, The Vogues, The Bachelors — but I really wanted to do it myself."

He did it himself with "Solitary Man", though ironically enough Neil didn't even want to record the self-penned song. "I wrote it just for myself," said Neil. "It was a personal thing to me and I didn't want to record it. After about three months of arguing I decided to do it."

... NEIL DIAMOND — Object of agency competition.

BARRY SADLER STARTS

The Sound of Being Alone

2

I'm searching for a tone and I haven't found it yet. I buy old upright pianos. I never spend more than $50 for them. Sometimes I just pay to have them moved. They really have the best tone. I've bought as many as 15 in one year. I'm supporting a moving company in New York. They're constantly moving them in and out because I only keep one piano at a time.

—Neil Diamond, early press release

The record that made Neil Diamond a rich man.

Bert Berns had a burgeoning résumé as a producer and songwriter. He did "Twist and Shout" with the Isley Brothers (and collected even more royalties when The Beatles covered it). He co-wrote "Piece of My Heart" (Janis Joplin) and created hit records with Solomon Burke ("Cry to Me"), the Drifters ("Under the Boardwalk"), and Them ("Here Comes the Night"). He also signed Them's short, red-haired singer, Van Morrison ("Brown Eyed Girl"), to Bang, as well as the McCoys ("Hang on Sloopy") and the Strangeloves ("I Want Candy"). The résumé shouted "great music man," but the reputation was stubborn, chart-obsessed businessman, as Neil Diamond would soon discover.

Neil's first single for Bang was "Solitary Man," which became a case of life imitating art. Diamond penned the tune in the new house on Long Island where he'd moved with his wife, Jaye (she added an "e" to her name by this time). "I wasn't trying to write anything about myself necessarily at the time," Diamond told the *Los Angeles Times* in 1992. "I thought it was just a

His pre-music jobs ranged from "delivery boy to delivery boy" until someone saw that glimmer and hired him to write songs for $30 or $40 a week.

—*Teen Set*, April 1967

New York City hotel room, circa 1967. *Photo by Roz Kelly/Michael Ochs Archives/Getty Images*

nice idea to write a song about a solitary guy. It wasn't until years later, when I went into Freudian analysis, that I understood that it was always me."

The song was inspired by the minor key of "Michelle" by The Beatles, he explained in 1996's *In My Lifetime*: "'Solitary Man' convinced me I'd always been this quiet, introverted kid. Then one of my fellow sixth-grade graduates came backstage recently and showed me our sixth-grade graduation book. I was shocked to be reminded that I had been voted 'most cheerful.' That totally shook my whole concept of what I was like as a child. I thought I was a loner and it turns out I was probably a cheerleader. On the other hand, 'Cheerful Man' wouldn't have sounded as good." Or made it to No. 55 on Billboard's pop chart.

Next came "Cherry, Cherry," which Jeff Barry once told England's *Melody Maker* magazine began

as "Money, Money," but he and Berns convinced Diamond to change the words. They also made a wise choice in deciding which version of "Cherry, Cherry" to release—the fully produced rendition with horns, backup vocals, and drums or the stripped-down demo with "simplicity and groove," as the singer put it. The demo treatment did the trick, climbing to No. 3 and bringing attention and opportunities for Diamond.

Impressed by this new smash single, Brill Building impresario Don Kirshner asked Diamond for material for the Monkees, his TV-concocted answer to The Beatles. Finally getting his opportunity as a songwriter, Diamond pulled out a trump card—his unreleased recording of "I'm a Believer." Kirshner thought it would fit the Monkees like a hand in a glove. He was right. Not only did their version spend seven weeks at No. 1, it was the biggest single of 1966. The next year, the Prefab Four went to No. 2 with another Diamond ditty, "A Little Bit Me, A Little Bit You."

While "I'm a Believer" made Diamond a rich man by selling six million copies, he admits that this first blush of songwriting success in the bubblegum vein was a little awkward. "That was right in the middle of The Beatles, and it was a little embarrassing for me," he told me in 1986. "It took me a couple years to live it down. I had to write 'Holly Holy' and 'Brother Love' and 'I Am . . . I Said' before people forgot about that."

Bang quickly put together Diamond's debut LP, *The Feel of Neil Diamond*, featuring his third hit, "I Got the Feelin' (Oh No No)," which he called "my first attempt to extend the emotional and stylistic range of my voice."

The hits from Bang kept on coming, most notably "Thank the Lord for the Night Time," which Diamond, writing the *In My Lifetime* liner notes, called "a rock and roll song with some black music influence . . . probably as close as this white Jewish kid from Brooklyn could come to being a gospel singer."

Gospel singer or not, Diamond was "always a total professional," recalled engineer Brooks Arthur, who worked on those Bang recordings. "He was very disciplined at a time when a lot of artists weren't very disciplined. He came to work completely prepared, and he usually had a lot of ideas about how things should go. He worked hard, and he was always very courteous to the musicians, the people in the studios, everybody." Speaking to *Mix Magazine* in October 1996, Arthur said Diamond displayed "confidence but never a swagger. Then and now, Neil is much too thoughtful of a man to have a swagger."

Even if he didn't have a swagger, Diamond had strong opinions about the marketing of his music. For the next single from his second album, *Just for You*, the singer favored "Shilo," but Berns insisted on "Kentucky Woman," which Diamond had written in the back of a limousine as he approached Paducah, Kentucky, during a Dick Clark Caravan (also featuring Tommy Roe, Billy Joe Royal, and P. J. Proby). Berns, the boss, prevailed, but Diamond left Bang with a convoluted lawsuit.

Bang Records promo poster, 1966.

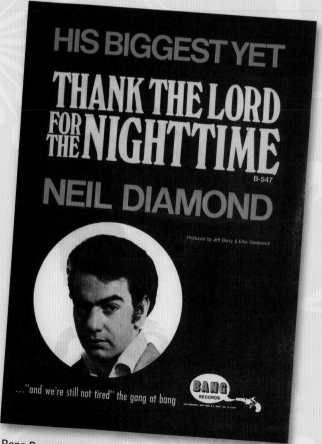

Bang Records promo poster, 1967.

Ronnie Dove's Neil-penned and produced "My Babe" b/w "Put My Mind at Ease," 1967.

For Diamond, 1967 was a very good year. The trade journal *Cash Box* declared that he tied Frank Sinatra as the year's No. 1 singer. However, the Brooklyn boy felt like a solitary man—a guy with a guitar in an era of bands, a star who headlined Carnegie Hall and no critics showed up. "It was like I didn't exist," he told *Rolling Stone* in 1988.

The star was having troubles on the home front, too. He and Jaye split up in 1968. They'd married too young, he told *Rolling Stone* in 1976. "It was almost as though our destiny was preordained. We were to be married, have children; the best we could hope for was a little house on Long Island. We'd live the lives our parents wanted us to live. I didn't really begin to think about myself and my life until I began to travel and remove myself from that peer group. And I realized that that wasn't what I wanted at all, and things began to deteriorate from that point. I just decided to split and leave it all behind. In a sense, it was running away."

He found solace in his new lady (TV production assistant Marcia Murphey), their move to Los Angeles, and a staggering $50,000-per-album, five-LP contract with MCA's Uni Records. However, not all was fine in L.A. "Brooklyn Roads," reflections of his childhood, became his first Uni single, but Bang decided to make its own noise with a new Neil single, "Shilo." Even Berns' death from a heart attack on December 31, 1967, didn't deter Bang. The label was determined to exploit all twenty-five songs Diamond recorded for them for years to come. "Shilo" fared better than "Brooklyn Roads" on the charts, reaching No. 24, but Diamond was delighted because "I loved the freedom of being able to write something without the charts in mind," he said in *In My Lifetime*.

While he had the artistic freedom, Diamond didn't have the commercial success. His Uni debut disc, *Velvet Gloves and Spit*, didn't even make Billboard's Top 200 list. In January 1969, he headed to Memphis to work with producer Chips Moman at American Sound Studios, where recent hits for the Box Tops and Dusty Springfield had been recorded and Elvis Presley was about to do some sessions for "In the Ghetto" and "Suspicious Minds." On the flight south, Diamond rewrote a set of lyrics to what would become "Brother Love's Traveling Salvation Show."

continued on page 41

Wichita, Kansas, November 21, 1967.

The Penthouse Presents

"The Association" and "Neil Diamond"

Tuesday, November 21, 8:30 P.M. at the W. S. U. Fieldhouse

Souvenir Program
.50¢

The Bitter End, New York, January 18–22, 1968. Photo by Michael Ochs Archives/Getty Images

One of the really good things about performing onstage is I'm never self-conscious. . . . That's the great thing about the stage. You don't have to watch it and worry about it. It's just a matter of doing it and experiencing and hoping the audience experiences it as well. That's one of my favorite things about the stage: I don't have to look back.

—Neil Diamond, 2008

These pages: Geauga Lake Park, Cleveland, Ohio, July 18, 1967. *Both photographed by George Shuba*

These pages: Radio station WIXY, Cleveland, Ohio, August 1968. *Both photographed by George Shuba*

continued from page 36

"The song was originally called 'Mo Getta Mo,' which has the same number of syllables as the 'love, brother, love' line," he told the *Los Angeles Times* in 1992. "It was just a groove with a fun chorus, but Marcia hated the title, and she kept bothering me to change it all the way on the flight to Memphis. I had been toying with the idea of writing a full concept album about a revival preacher, so I rewrote the entire lyric of the song on the plane. It's basically an entire album concept condensed into one song. And it's special because it gave me a closer to my [stage] show."

A couple of months later, before another recording session in Memphis, Diamond needed another song for the next day. In his hotel room, he grabbed his guitar and penned "Sweet Caroline," which, he finally admitted in 2007, was inspired by a photo of eleven-year-old Caroline Kennedy, the daughter of the late President John Kennedy. That little late-night number would not only become Diamond's most covered song—everyone from Elvis and Sinatra to Waylon Jennings and Ray Conniff cut a version—but a special eighth-inning anthem at Boston Red Sox games at Fenway Park, starting in the late 1990s (and depicted in the 2005 Jimmy Fallon/Drew Barrymore film, *Fever Pitch*).

Those Memphis sessions also produced another Diamond classic, "Holly Holy," which he wrote while his infant son Jesse was sleeping in the next room. "What I tried to do," he told the BBC, "was to create a religious experience between a man and a woman, as opposed to a man and a god."

Despite his made-in-Memphis hits, Diamond was a music-biz outcast in Los Angeles. Rock stars reveling in the counterculture and antiwar movement ruled the scene. "I never could identify with that. I never did understand . . . this rebelliousness," he said in the 1976 *Rolling Stone* interview. "It didn't relate to what I was trying to do, which was essentially to try and be Alan Jay Lerner or George Gershwin. Hip was something

frivolous people had time to be. I didn't have time to be hip and with it and groovy. I was dealing with something that was much more important: with my life and trying to write songs that had substance. And hip is bullshit. It doesn't cut deep. It cuts for today and tomorrow. I suppose from a business point of view I could have tried to be hip. The growing of the beard [see the *Brother Love* LP cover], I suppose, from outward appearances, looked like I was getting hip or something. In reality, I was hiding from some private detectives my first wife had hired."

A month after tying the knot with Marcia on December 4, 1969, Neil recorded the first in what was to become a series of live albums. This one was simple. Named *Gold*, it was recorded at the Troubadour, a legendary Hollywood folk club on Santa Monica Boulevard, and he was backed by his three touring musicians and three female backup singers.

continued on page 44

Japan, 1967.

悲しきプロフィール

●●GIRL, YOU'LL BE A WOMAN SOON●●●●YOU'LL FORGET●●●

ユール・フォーゲット / ☆ニール・ダイアモンド

SR-1712

Stateside
RECORDS

東芝音楽工業株式会社 © ¥370

Portugal, circa 1970.

sweet caroline
..... dig in

neil diamond

France, 1969.

Holland, circa 1970.

Turkey, circa 1970.

NEIL DIAMOND
SOLITARY MAN
Soolaimon

SOLITARY MAN
NEIL DIAMOND
THE TIME IS NOW

PINK ELEPHANT

NEIL DIAMOND
SOLITARY MAN 2'28
(Neil Diamond)
Produced by Jeff Barry & Ellie Greenwich
This is a original Bang record

PE 22.528Y
DU 21643
60

continued from page 41

But before *Gold* was released, Diamond delivered his most ambitious and adventurous album yet: *Tap Root Manuscript*.

The catchy "Cracklin' Rosie" was inspired by an Indian reservation in Canada on which men outnumbered women. "On a Saturday night, those men left alone would buy a bottle of Crackling Rosie wine, and that bottle became their woman for the night," he explained in *In My Lifetime*.

Another track from *Tap Root*, "He Ain't Heavy, He's My Brother" was a Bobby Scott/Bob Russell composition that the Hollies had released in late 1969. Diamond's own "Done Too Soon" was a musical survey of important people who'd died young, including Jesus Christ, Fanny Brice, John Wilkes Booth, and Karl Marx.

And then there was "Soolaimon" from the "African Trilogy" suite, which filled one side of the LP. Through the United Nations and the African studies department at UCLA, Diamond researched African music and came up with this left-field, out-of-Africa hit. "The title is meant to be a variation of the word *salamah*, meaning 'hello and welcome' as well as 'goodbye and peace be with you,' in many languages," the songwriter explained in *In My Lifetime*. With *Tap Root Manuscript*, Diamond was just beginning to tap into new pop music possibilities. ✦

The first two Diamond compilations, *Greatest Hits* (1968) and *Shilo* (1970).

Q: How much do you smoke?
A: As much as I can. At least two packs a day.

—Neil Diamond, 1986

Opening night, Winter Garden Theatre, New York City, October 3, 1972. *Photo by Michael Mauney/Time Life Pictures/Getty Images*

Lonely Looking Sky

3

I've probably been to four bars in my life, to maybe three nightclubs. I don't drink. It doesn't matter really where I go, I generally just get into myself, think about things. Sometimes I come up with answers. Sometimes answers come quickly. Sometimes it takes years. Sometimes I'm just left hanging. But when I *do* find something, something real, it all pays off. Because I know then that that truth, that love, that vision is mine and mine alone.

—Neil Diamond, early-1970s press release

It is, he says, his best composition. "I Am . . . I Said" took forever—well, four months—to write. He hatched the idea while doing a screen test for a movie about acerbic, foul-mouthed social-commentator/comedian Lenny Bruce. Diamond had performed one of the scenes in the morning and retreated to his dressing room for lunch.

"I was really depressed 'cause I knew I had done a miserable job," Diamond told author David Wild in his 2008 book *He Is . . . I Say*. "I had my guitar there, and I started to play this thing, which within fifteen minutes started to have a title. And it had the line about the frog who dreamed about being a king. So I went in every day and fought it. . . . It took four months every day, all day. I'd go into my room, lock the door and I struggled with this song. I cursed it out. It was like a person who wouldn't submit. I got as close as I could go."

Was it worth the struggle? Of course. "It was by far the most difficult song I have ever written, and probably the best song I have ever written," he declared in 1992 to the *Los Angeles Times*.

Trade ads, 1970.

If self-doubt gnawed at Neil during the battle to put the raw truth into lyrics for "I Am . . . I Said," the audition to play the First Amendment–waving, no-holds-barred rebel Bruce drove him to see a shrink. "I went into therapy almost immediately after that," he told *Rolling Stone* in 1976. "Because there were things coming out of me that I couldn't deal with. It was frightening because I had never been willing to admit this part of my personality."

Diamond didn't get the movie role; in fact, the project was never made. (However, in 1974, director Bob Fosse cast Dustin Hoffman in *Lenny*, which earned Hoffman an Academy Award nomination for best actor.) But Diamond's pop career didn't miss a beat. "Song Sung Blue" from 1972's *Moods* became his first No. 1 single. True to form, Diamond had doubts about "the very simple, very light, easygoing" song being a single. He told Russ Regan, the head of Uni Records, that "Play Me" would be the payoff. Regan insisted on "Song Sung Blue." "Even though I didn't realize it at the time, I feel now that I probably said more in less words than in any other song I've written," Diamond explained about "Song Sung Blue" to the *Los Angeles Times* in 1992. "That's one of the fascinating things about songwriting. How you can write a song like 'Sweet Caroline' and 'Song Sung Blue' so fast and then have to struggle so long on 'I Am . . . I Said'? You never know where a song is going to come from. You can just be sitting there and suddenly the most extraordinary thing pops out. That's what every songwriter waits for."

continued on page 54

The Johnny Cash Show, airdate September 30, 1970.

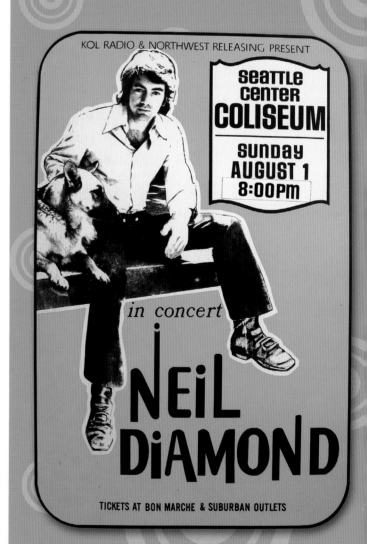

Coliseum, Seattle, Washington, August 1, 1971.
Courtesy Pete Howard, postercentral.com

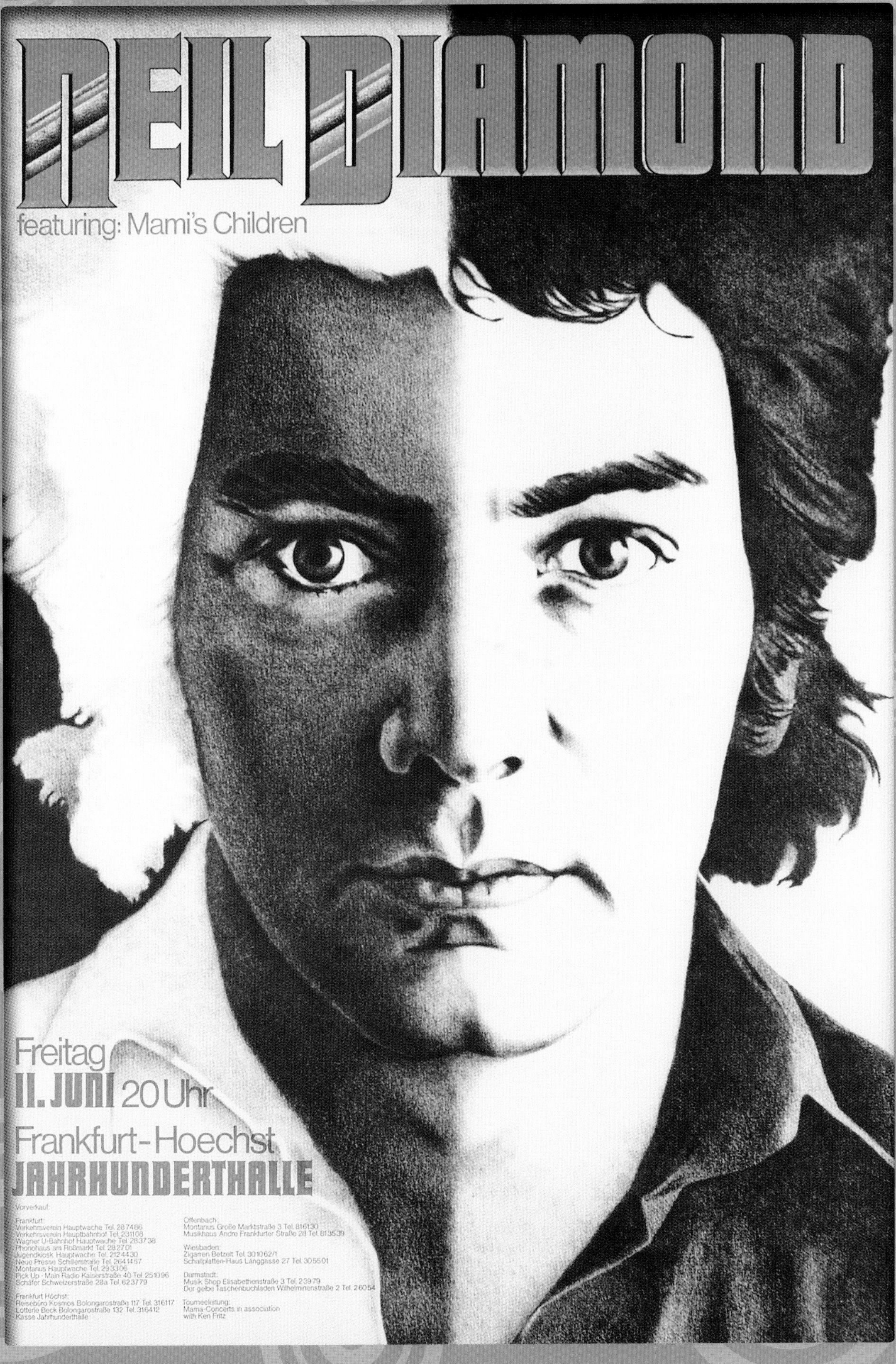

Jahrhunderthalle, Frankfurt, June 11, 1971.

France, 1971.

1er chanteur MONDIAL
classé par The National Association of Recorded Music
U.S.A. 1971

PHILIPS

**NEIL
DIAMOND**

"I AM...I SAID"

b/w "DONE TOO SOON"

6073 03T
(MC/S 5432)

UNI

**Neil
Diamond**

STONES
Crunchy Granola

Holland, 1971.

073 023
stereo

UNI

**Sweet
Caroline**

I Am
The Lion

**Neil
Diamond**

Germany, 1971.

PHILIPS

6098 006
(MCS 4580)

série
PARADE

45

MONO

1

I AM... I SAID (N. Diamond) 3:30
NEIL DIAMOND
arranged by Marty Paich and Larry Mahoberac
produced by Tom Catalano
Licensed by MCA Records International
A division of MCA Inc.
New-York, USA

APRIL 7-8PM-MOBY GYM-TICKETS $5,$4,$3 AT S.C. BOX OFFICE S.E.B PRESENTS:

CSU

NEIL DIAMOND

ROBERT QUALLY

Chess in Kensington Gardens, England, before
a nineteen-date European tour, May 25, 1972.
Photo by Popperfoto/Getty Images

ROYAL ALBERT HALL
General Manager: FRANK J. MUNDY

Saturday, 27 May, 1972
at 7.30 p.m.   Doors open at 7

Arthur Howes presents
NEIL DIAMOND

BALCONY R £1.00

ROW 5

SEAT 62

Enter by
Door No. 5

TO BE RETAINED

NO RE-ADMISSION

MCA's Diana Ross & The Supremes/
Neil Diamond Motown/Uni split release, 1972.

Fabric sticker from Holland.

NEIL DIAMOND

continued from page 48

Prior to releasing *Moods*, Diamond declared it time to renegotiate his contract with MCA Records. A bidding war ensued between Warner Bros. and Columbia Records. Money talked, and Diamond opted for the latter's record $4 million, ten-album deal. In 1972, he lived large, recording *Hot August Night* with a thirty-five-piece orchestra during an unprecedented ten-night engagement at Hollywood's Greek Theatre and breaking ground on Broadway with twenty sold-out shows at the Winter Garden Theatre. *The New York Times* called it "a brash idea. One-man shows have traditionally been associated with monster talents like the Judy Garlands and Danny Kayes. . . . But Mr. Diamond is clearly a brash young man, and one with both the musical track record and the performance macho to bring it off. In presence, command on the stage, timing and self-confidence, he needn't worry about comparisons with the likes of Miss Garland and Mr. Kaye."

continued on page 58

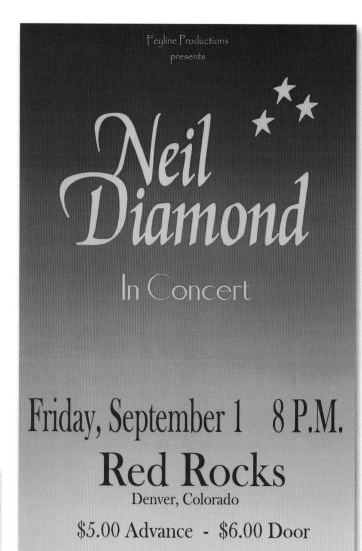

Neil played his famous ten sold-out concerts at the Greek Theatre in Los Angeles just prior to this 1972 show in Denver. Due to inclement weather, the performance was moved from Red Rocks to the indoor Denver Coliseum.

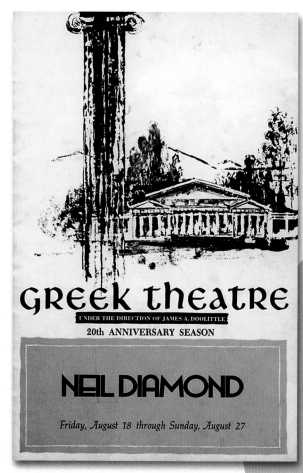

Program, Greek Theatre, August 18–27, 1972.

When I think of Neil Diamond

I just think of that picture from that live album where he had that denim suit on and he's holding the mic stand like a twelve-foot [expletive] protruding out between his legs . . . there was something incredibly huge and rock about that picture. I've never been able to shed that image. I think Rick [Rubin] has in some ways brought out the best in him on the last couple of records.

—Lars Ulrich, Metallica, 2008

Hot August
Night
Greek '72

Karin Thieme
Nw. 27, 2000

One of a series of watercolors executed by Karin Thieme based on Ed Caraeff's photography of the August 1972 Greek Theatre shows. *Courtesy of Karin Thieme*

The Shubert Organization presents

NEIL DIAMOND

THE WINTER GARDEN THEATRE
Broadway at 50th Street
Previews Oct. 3 & 4 - Opens Oct. 5-21

Playbill covering
Neil's legendary Winter
Garden engagement.
Courtesy Karin Thieme collection

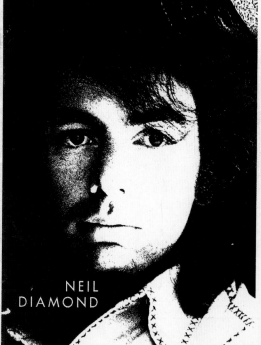

Neil played twenty sold-out shows at New York City's Winter Garden Theatre
in October 1972. He didn't tour again until 1976.

Opening night of the twenty-show residency at Winter Garden Theatre, New York City, October 3, 1972.
Photo by Ron Galella/WireImage

continued from page 54

While on Broadway, the hopelessly driven Diamond threw Columbia a curveball: He was going to take a sabbatical from touring.

"I felt I had to get away from the traveling for a while," he told me in 1976. "Settle down, put some roots down, catch up on some very ordinary, average things that most people take for granted, like getting up in the morning and having breakfast in your own home, reading the newspaper, walking your dog at night, going to a film when you feel like it, visiting with friends, catching up on a great deal of reading, getting to know your family again, establishing friendships, being able to socialize generally. These are things I feel I missed out on traveling and working exclusively on the music. So I decided to take a short sabbatical. I thought at most it would last two years. It was closer to four. What I did during that period of time is essentially what I set out to do. A great deal of reading, I made some new friends. I read everything you could possibly think of. *Zen and the Art of Motorcycle Maintenance*, *The Lives of a Cell*, autobiographies of other composers—George Gershwin, Cole Porter, et cetera. Something like a hundred or hundred-fifty books. I just devoured it. It was like a college education for me."

During the touring sabbatical, Diamond continued to make recordings. But the first album was another curveball for Columbia: a soundtrack for a movie based on a bestselling book about a bird, *Jonathan Livingston Seagull*. Director-producer Hall Bartlett (*All the Young Men* and *Zero Hour*) had seen Diamond in concert at the Greek Theatre and invited him to write music for *Seagull*. "I didn't have the vaguest idea how to write songs from a seagull's point of view," Diamond wrote in *In My Lifetime*. "So I turned it down. Then I thought a little more and decided to do it. I figured nobody else

Winter Garden Theatre, October 1972. *Photo by Michael Mauney/Time Life Pictures/Getty Images*

had more insight into writing for seagull, so why not?" Plus, like the bird, the spiritual Diamond was kind of the black sheep of the flock.

In fact, the singer, who had traveled from the revival tent of "Brother Love" to the self-help of "I Am . . . I Said," was becoming increasingly spiritual and philosophical. He was even open to a Hare Krishna who knocked on his door to give him literature. "I invited him in. We talked for a while, and I asked him to read the [*Seagull*] script and tell me what he thought of it, had him make notes on it," Diamond told *Family Weekly* in February 1976. "I wound up working with him about six weeks. Put him up in an apartment, rented him a car, until I reached the point where I had to work alone on it. He wanted me to go off with him

continued on page 62

With Ethel Kennedy, Winter Garden Theatre, October 1972. A portion of the proceeds from the opening show of the twenty-night stand went to a memorial fund for Robert F. Kennedy. *Photo by Michael Mauney/Time Life Pictures/Getty Images*

Neil shows his fencing form, October 1972. *Photo by Michael Mauney/Time Life Pictures/Getty Images*

I had secretly hoped when I finished at the Winter Garden that I would never have to come back and perform. I was exhausted. But then I got itchy about wanting to be in front of an audience again. I wanted to test myself again.

— Neil Diamond *Los Angeles Times,* February 15, 1976

Portugal, 1972.

Q: What's your most satisfying song?

A: Onstage I'd have to say "Brother Love." Listening at home on the phonograph, I'd probably say "Play Me," "I Am . . . I Said" or "Morningside."

—Neil Diamond

DJ promo singles.

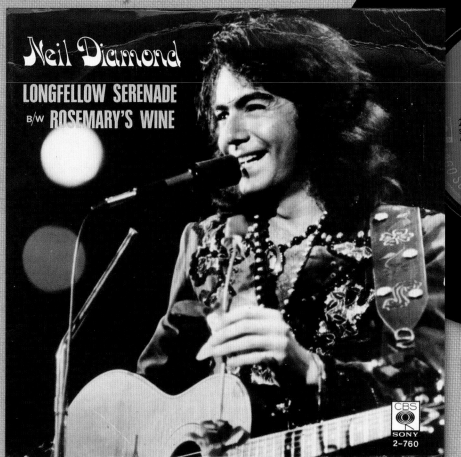

Mexico, 1973.

Malaysia, 1974.

continued from page 58

to India and sit in a cave. I said that sounded great and I'd love to, but now I had to write this thing. I gave him a plane ticket, and he went while I settled down to pull it all together."

Diamond also consulted noted film score composers Henry Mancini and Lalo Schifrin, but ultimately it came down to putting his own soul-searching into music. "The process itself—the writing and the understanding that you had to come to—was also an interesting part of my life, and also reflects part of my idea of self-improvement and, you know, moving on and not necessarily traveling with the flock. It was a great experience."

In his 1987 warts-and-all book *Neil Diamond: Solitary Star*, Rich Wiseman makes it sound as if this was a torturous task for the composer. Apparently, Bartlett wanted Diamond to be the voice of Jonathan, and they argued over this issue, royalties, and credits. The off-camera intrigue may have been more compelling than the film itself.

The movie about this soul-searching bird went over like a lead zeppelin. Richard Bach, the author of the book, sued to block its release. Roger Ebert, the Chicago film critic, admitted in his review that he walked out long before it was over. But Diamond's soundtrack soared like a flock of seagulls, becoming

one of his bestselling albums and earning him his first—and thus far only—Grammy Award, for best instrumental composition for a movie or television.

Like the film, Diamond's soundtrack took a beating from critics. Three years after the movie was released, I asked him, "The movie was dismissed by critics as maudlin, platitudinous fluff. Some critics have said similar things about your work, calling it pretentious and without humor. How do you react to that?" Diamond replied, "Sometimes it is, you know. Some of it is being accepted by some of the people. It's all of those things. It's other things, too."

From the *Seagull* project, Diamond had one song he hadn't quite finished, "I've Been This Way Before." A piece about reincarnation, it gives its composer a feeling of the glass being half empty. "A lot of people say this is one of their favorites, but I've always felt a sense of disappointment in that song," he said in 1992 to the *Los Angeles Times*, "because I wrote it for the *Jonathan Livingston Seagull* movie and didn't finish it in time to get it on the album. It was supposed to be the concluding statement." Instead it became the first song on 1974's *Serenade*, on which he used some famous figures to build the hit "Longfellow Serenade" and "The Last Picasso." ✦

With BBC Radio 1 disc jockey Tony Blackburn, December 1974.
Photo by Sydney O'Meara/Evening Standard/Getty Images

Photo by GEMS/Redferns

It's the Sound
That I Love

4

I have never understood the kind of artist who thinks he has some kind of divine right to play and the audience has to work to get inside what he's trying to communicate.

—Neil Diamond, *Melody Maker*, April 23, 1977

Robbie Robertson, the leader of the hip, rootsy Band, and Neil Diamond, the uncrowned king of pop, first met in 1972 in Woodstock, New York, the haven for hipsters. Now they'd reconnected two years later as neighbors in Malibu, California, where Diamond had a home and Robertson was working with Bob Dylan. The hipster and the un-hip sat on the beach and talked about music, life, and making an album together.

Like almost everyone in the United States, Robertson knew Diamond's music from the radio. "The main thing was trying to understand whether the experiment would work musically," Robertson told *Rolling Stone* in 1976. "It seemed just weird enough that it was a worthwhile undertaking."

The Robertson-produced *Beautiful Noise* was Diamond's first album to receive widespread critical acclaim. Was it the depth and range of the beautiful noises on the record or the "Produced by Robbie Robertson" imprimatur on the cover? Whatever it was, this odd couple from two different musical camps created something that belonged in an entity of its own.

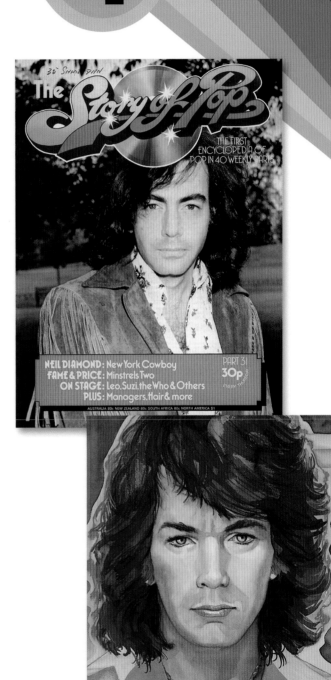

Children's book, Creative Educational Society, Mankato, Minnesota, 1975.
Cover illustration by John Keely

Uruguayan greatest hits compilation.

Lado 1:
1. DULCE CAROLINA
(Sweet Caroline)
2. HOLLY HOLY
3. Y EL CANTANTE CANTA SU CANCION
(And the singer sings his song)
4. SHILO
5. INTERPRETAME
(Play me)
6. SR. BOJANGLES
(Mr. Bojangles)
7. CANTANDO UNA TRISTE CANCION
(Song sung blue)
8. CHERRY CHERRY
9. HOMBRE SOLITARIO
(Solitary man)
10. MUJER DE KENTUCKY
(Kentucky woman)

Lado 2:
1. CRACKLIN' ROSIE
2. SOOLAIMON
3. CANTA LIBRE
4. PIEDRAS
(Stones)
5. NO ME PESA . . . ES MI HERMANO
(He ain't heavy he's my brother)
6. EL SHOW DE SALVACION VIAJERO
DEL HERMANO AMOR
(Brother love's travelling
salvation show)
7. AGUA FRIA DE LA MAÑANA
(Cold water morning)
8. CAMINA SOBRE EL AGUA
(Walk on water)
9. Y LA HIERBA NO HARA CASO
(And the grass won't pay no mind)
10. YO SOY YO DIJE
(I am I said)

Todos los temas compuestos por NEIL DIAMOND,
excepto No me pesa . . . es mi hermano - Russell-Scott
y Sr. Bojangles - Walker

DISCO ES CULTURA

PRODUCTOR FONOGRAFICO EDISA · Montevideo · Uruguay
Art. 79 de la Ley 13-349 D.L. 146-352/79 IMP. FIMASA
Reservado todo derecho del Productor Fonográfico y de los Autores de las obras gra
en este disco contenido en este sobre, prohibida su reproducción, o grabación, pu
privada, y la ejecución pública por cualquier usuario y procedimiento.

"I think an album of twelve folk tunes with guitar and cello would be kind of dull. I like to work in different forms. It gives me a chance to experiment and play around with things," Diamond told me when the album was released. "Also on this project, it represented a lot of different characters and moods and situations. Reflecting 'Street Life,' it seemed natural to work with a hot street funky jazz thing. 'Stargazer' was old-timer advice given to me by an old-time songwriter, and that old-time Dixieland jazz thing was more appropriate."

The title track was sparked by a visit with Diamond's two daughters (Marjorie and Elyn, from his first marriage) at the Sherry-Netherland Hotel in New York City. The girls were coloring with their dad.

"There was a Puerto Rican Day parade going by with all sorts of bands in it," Diamond told the *Los Angeles Times* in 1992. "My daughter Marjorie looked out the window and said, 'What a beautiful noise,' and it just hit me like a bolt. I ran over and wrote it down. My parents were there, and I just sang the song into a tape recorder."

"Dry Your Eyes" was a tune he wrote with Robertson. "It's basically the story of the sixties generation and what they lost . . . their innocence and heroes," Diamond told the *L.A. Times*. "It's a sad song, and I've only done it once in concert; at *The Last Waltz* show in San Francisco. I don't know why I don't do it more. Maybe I should."

Times Square, New York City, 1976. *Photo by Waring Abbott/Michael Ochs Archives/Getty Images*

The Last Waltz was an iconic concert movie, directed by Martin Scorsese, and a curious moment for Diamond. Billed as a farewell concert for The Band, it featured a parade of rock stars—Bob Dylan, Eric Clapton, Neil Young, Van Morrison, Joni Mitchell, Dr. John, Ringo Starr, Joe Cocker, Stephen Stills, Ron Wood, and Muddy Waters. And then there was Neil Diamond. Some of the stars, including members of The Band, were puzzled by the pop star's inclusion. But during The Last Waltz, Robertson hailed "Dry Your Eyes" as a "great song." The audience at Winterland Ballroom in San Francisco didn't boo or react negatively, but the response was hardly as excited as it was for Morrison's leg-kicking rendition of "Caravan."

One of the oddities of being there was that after every couple of performances the show stopped for several minutes so Scorsese's people could change film. That made for a lot of pregnant pauses at what would become a historic event.

Legend has it that when Diamond came off stage he facetiously said to Dylan, "You'll have to be pretty good to follow me," to which Dylan retorted, "What do I have to do, go on stage and fall asleep?"

In 1992, I asked Diamond if he felt out of place at The Last Waltz. "I did feel a little out of place because there were so many stars around there that I felt, you know, there were a lot of folk people and people I hadn't met before, although I know Bob Dylan and I know a couple of the other people," he said. "I knew Robbie, and Neil Young came over and introduced himself as Neil Sedaka. I know Joni Mitchell. I felt a little out of place. But Robbie asked me to come do it. In the middle of Thanksgiving dinner, I flew up to San Francisco, did my song, flew down, and finished Thanksgiving dinner with my kids. And that's the whole story."

continued on page 74

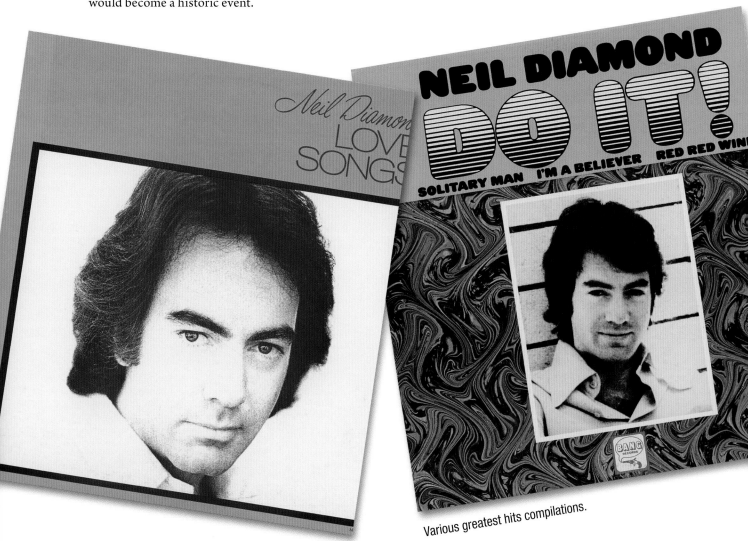

Various greatest hits compilations.

Neil Diamond's one of the greatest artists of all time. . . . That guy's written some of the simplest, greatest pop tunes, just so soulful. My best Neil Diamond story is that, back when The Band did *The Last Waltz*, I was there, in the audience. Back then I wasn't a Neil Diamond fan for sure; he was way too pop and old school for me. But when he came on stage he just blew my mind. He blew everybody off the stage that night. He was so charismatic. Ever since that moment I've been a Neil Diamond fan.

—**Sammy Hagar**

Honolulu, Hawaii.

At *The Last Waltz* with, from left, Dr. John, Joni Mitchell, Neil Young, Rick Danko, Van Morrison, Bob Dylan, and Robbie Robertson. Winterland Ballroom, San Francisco, November 25, 1976. *United Artists/The Kobal Collection*

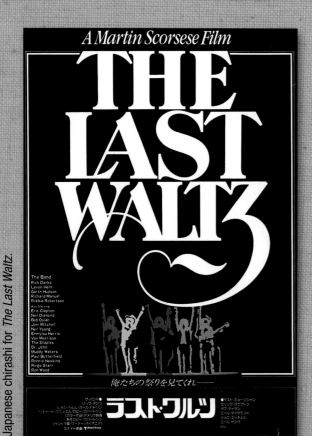

Japanese chirashi for *The Last Waltz.*

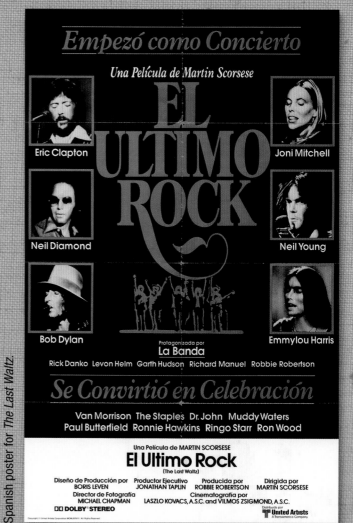

Spanish poster for *The Last Waltz.*

Circa 1976. *Photo by Michael Ochs Archives/Getty Images*

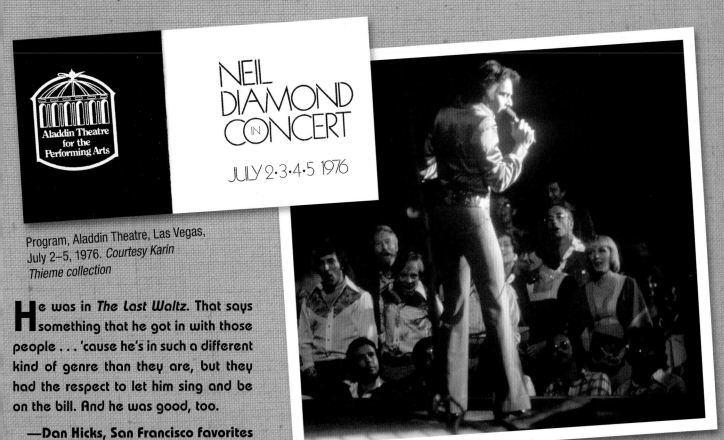

Program, Aladdin Theatre, Las Vegas, July 2–5, 1976. *Courtesy Karin Thieme collection*

He was in *The Last Waltz*. That says something that he got in with those people . . . 'cause he's in such a different kind of genre than they are, but they had the respect to let him sing and be on the bill. And he was good, too.

—Dan Hicks, San Francisco favorites Dan Hicks & The Hot Licks

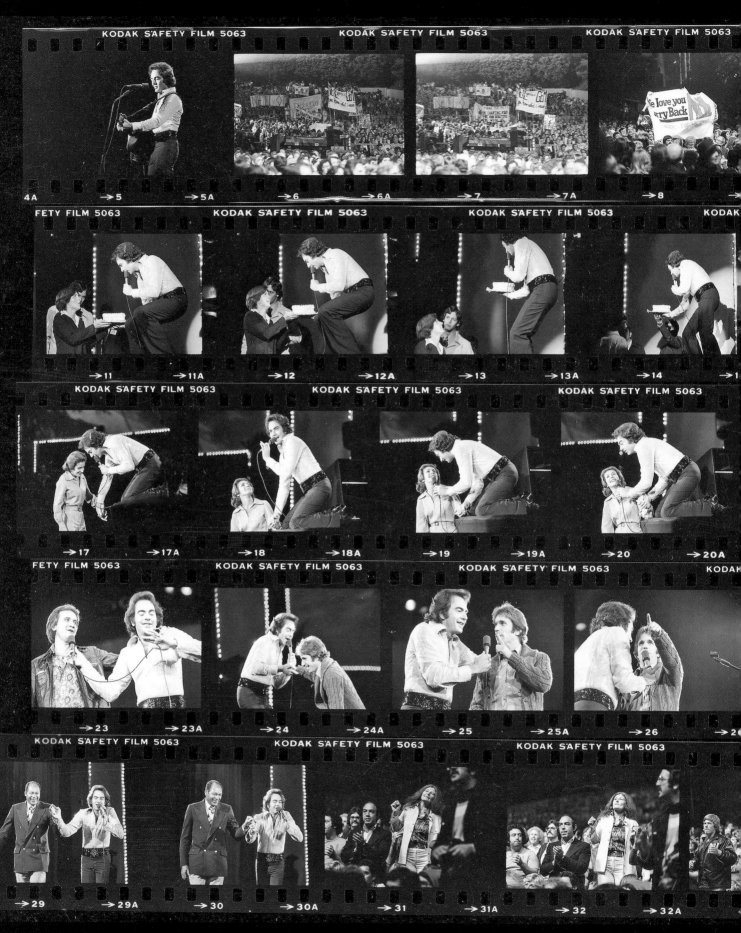

Contact sheet from Greek Theatre, Los Angeles, September 1976, depicting Neil, Helen Reddy, Roger Miller, Henry Winkler, and Mayor Tom Bradley. *Photo by Michael Ochs Archives/Getty Images*

Greek Theatre, Los Angeles, eight-show stand, September 13–20, 1976. *Photo by Michael Ochs Archives/Getty Images*

Greek Theatre, Los Angeles, eight-show stand, September 13–20, 1976. *Photo by Michael Ochs Archives/Getty Images*

continued from page 68

Part of the Neil Diamond story in 1976 involves the impact of the therapy he underwent during his sabbatical from touring. He reflected upon it during an interview with me:

Q: Talk about your therapy and how it affected your music and career.

A: I went through some psychological therapy for about three years. It was fascinating for me. It taught me how to verbalize things. To talk, to be able to express myself without holding back, without clamming up, without building up walls around myself, without being self protective. It was really impossible for me to communicate with people on a level other than on a musical level. In that sense, it was a tremendous growth experience for me.

Q: How has that affected your music?

A: In that I understand myself a lot better now. It's resulted in changes in the music. Lyrically, [it's] probably deeper and more sensitive to what's going on in people's heads, myself included. There's no question that it's changed me. It's made me a happier person so there's more joy in making music for me now.

Q: I read in an interview that you discovered yourself during this therapy. Who is Neil Diamond?

A: He's a guy with aspirations, with hopes of really doing something useful with his life, hopes of being able to give as much as he can. I'd like to make a contribution somehow. Right now it's my music. I feel very satisfied to be able to do it in that way. But I'm a man of very simple values; very basic values. Good friends, loving family, devotion and dedication to my work and the joy of what I do. These are the things that sustain me and give me reason to get up every morning and go out and face a rather complicated and difficult world.

Circa 1977. *GAB Archives/Redferns Collection/Getty Images*

At the Academy Awards, March 28, 1977, with Paul Williams and Barbra Streisand, who won an Oscar for Best Original Song with "Evergreen (Love Theme from *A Star Is Born*)." Neil presented the award.
© Armondo Gallo/Retna Ltd.

[Barbra and I] didn't know each other in high school but we sang in the same chorus for two years together at Erasmus Hall High School in Brooklyn. Years later we met in Los Angeles and realized we did sing in the same chorus and we had a lot of laughs over some of the stories of how all the girls were in love with the conductor, a very handsome Italian man. And all of the boys were deathly afraid of him because he was a tyrant. But that's where we both started.

—Neil Diamond, 1996

Neil also is a man who needs to be onstage. He used a fencing analogy to explain his desire to get back on tour. "In fencing there's a thing called blade hunger," he told me. "That really describes a fencer sitting on the sideline watching a bout between two other fencers. Blade hunger infers the anticipation of getting into the battle. So I suppose that I caught a severe case of blade hunger a year ago and just decided that I had the juices and enthusiasm for it and wanted to get back out and show everybody what I could do."

Diamond returned to the road in a big way with his Las Vegas debut at the brand-new Aladdin Theatre for the Performing Arts ($650,000 for five sold-out shows, each in front of 7,500 people) and a tour resulting in the *Neil Diamond: Love at the Greek* television special and another live double LP, *Love at the Greek*, featuring such new bandmembers as pianist Tom Hensley, percussionist King Errisson, guitarist Doug Rhone, and backup singer Linda Press.

While Robertson produced the live album, Diamond turned to Bob Gaudio, the composer/producer for the Four Seasons, for his next studio album. *I'm Glad You're Here with Me Tonight* featured a title song co-written by Gaudio and his wife, Judy Parker, and a Diamond collaboration with famed lyricists Alan and Marilynn Bergman written at the behest of television super-producer Norman Lear. Neil was sitting next to Norman at George Burns' eightieth birthday party and asked what brilliant new show needed a brilliant theme song. It turned out that the genius behind *All in the Family* was looking for a song for *All That Glitters*, a sitcom in which the traditional male/female roles are reversed. The three songwriters came up with "You Don't Bring Me Flowers."

Barbra Streisand, who'd often recorded material by the Bergmans, cut a version of the song, and radio DJs around the country began splicing the Babs and Neil readings together into one song. Neil picked up the story in 1992:

"Coincidentally, we sang it in the same key, so it lent itself to be cut together and made into a duet. I had four or five tapes from disc jockeys. I heard it,

continued on page 81

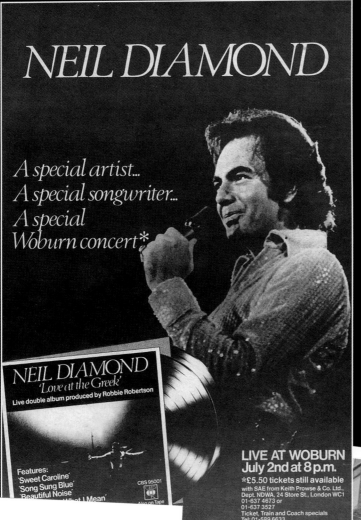

NEIL DIAMOND

A special artist...
A special songwriter...
A special
Woburn concert*

NEIL DIAMOND
'Love at the Greek'
Live double album produced by Robbie Robertson

Features:
'Sweet Caroline'
'Song Sung Blue'
'Beautiful Noise'
...What I Mean'

CBS 95001
Also on Tape

LIVE AT WOBURN
July 2nd at 8 p.m.
*£5.50 tickets still available
with SAE from Keith Prowse & Co. Ltd.,
Dept. NDWA, 24 Store St., London WC1
01-637 4673 or
01-637 3527
Ticket, Train and Coach specials
Tel: 01-589 6633

Woburn Abbey, Bedfordshire, England, July 2, 1977.

ROBERT PATERSON
presents   06084

NEIL DIAMOND

WOBURN ABBEY
JULY 2nd at 8 p.m.

Open-air.   Rear-block seat.   £7.

All seats unreserved. Please arrive early
Concert area opens 5 p.m.

No refund on cancellation due to weather conditions
or circumstances beyond the promoter's control.

Meeting fans before the show at Woburn Abbey,
Bedfordshire, England, July 2, 1977. Photo by
Tom Sheehan/Sony Music Archive/Getty Images

CHE SARA SARA

Neil Diamond at Woburn Abbey

Saturday July 2 1977

Woburn Abbey program, July 2, 1977.
Courtesy Karin Thieme collection

November 17, 1977.

Fan photo, Indianapolis, Indiana, August 2, 1978.

Three times [Diamond] went through the preliminaries of doing a TV special and three times he stopped, at a cost of about $300,000 to himself, because he didn't feel it was right.

—The Indianapolis News, February 19, 1977

It's the Sound That I Love

大空に歌おう

LET ME TAKE YOU IN MY ARMS

ニール・ダイアモンド
NEIL DIAMOND
c/w ロングフェロー・セレナーデ（ライブ）
LONGFELLOW SERENADE (LIVE)

キリンビール
CMソング

¥600

Japan, 1977.

Q: Why do you strive so hard to be accepted?

A: Uh, I suppose because I have a need for it. Where that need came from, I'm not sure. But there is a need for it. I'm driven by some kind of vague sense of finding perfection in what I do. I'm beginning more and more to realize that it's an impossible goal but again it is a goal. Even when I fall short of it, at least I'm able to feel that I've given it my best shot.

—Neil Diamond, 1976

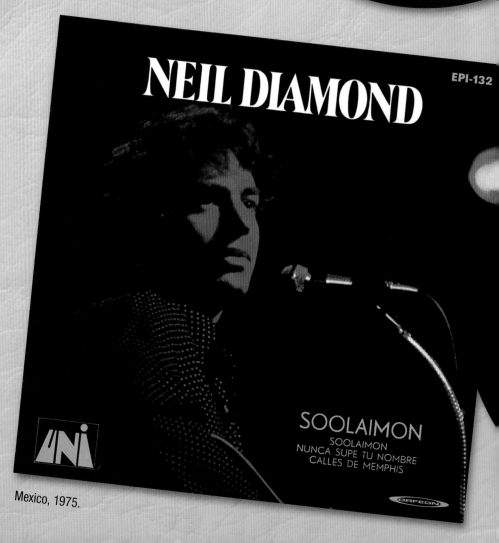

NEIL DIAMOND

EPI-132

SOOLAIMON
SOOLAIMON
NUNCA SUPE TU NOMBRE
CALLES DE MEMPHIS

Mexico, 1975.

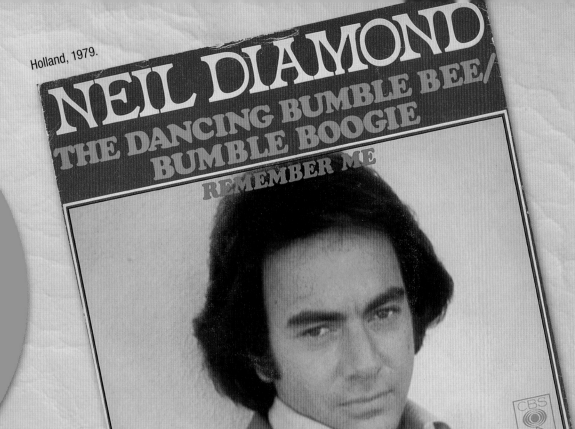

Holland, 1979.

NEIL DIAMOND
THE DANCING BUMBLE BEE/
BUMBLE BOOGIE
REMEMBER ME

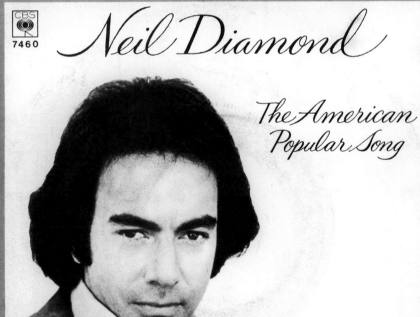

DJ promo, Germany, 1978.

Photo by Darryl Pitt/Retna Ltd.

After back surgery, rehearsing in Los Angeles for 1979 concert dates. Photo by George Rose/Getty Images

continued from page 75

and I liked it a lot. Who wouldn't like themselves in a duet with Barbra Streisand? She's only the greatest. Her people or management was hesitant about it. CBS [Columbia Records' parent company] was hesitant. They threatened to sue the disc jockeys, and then I threatened to sue CBS, and they sued the disc jockeys. I said, 'If you guys are smart, you'll get me and Barbra in the studio.' This was after her record came out. Barbra and I were both willing. We recorded one song. We didn't have a B-side; we put the instrumental version on the B-side. And it was a No. 1 record, for some reason, in most of the civilized world. So out of the blue. Totally unlike anything on the radio."

Streisand wasn't the only big shot tied to *You Don't Bring Me Flowers*. Diamond enlisted movie director William Friedkin of *The Exorcist* and *The French Connection* fame to direct a television special centered on a concert at Woburn Abbey in London. The show carried the same title as the album.

In 1979, Diamond offered *September Morn*, an album featuring a few songs co-written with French entertainer Gilbert Bécaud, who had been captivated by Neil's performance in Paris. Diamond was torn between two ballads he'd written for the project, so he gave Columbia Records a choice: "Hello Again" or "September Morn." They opted for the latter. Diamond saved the former for a movie project he was contemplating. But first there was a trip to the hospital to deal with back pain and numbness in his right leg. A twelve-hour surgery took care of a benign tumor compressing his spinal cord. He spent three months in a wheelchair, *Time* magazine reported, "uncertain if he would ever walk again." ✦

The Ultimate
Bar Mitzvah

5

It's very difficult to read something in the newspaper that's negative. It's always hard to swallow. But you have to accept it. If you want to accept the positive things, you have to accept the negative things as well. For the most part, the press has been good to me. I really have no complaints. If it all turned around and everybody got down on me, it would be very difficult.

—Neil Diamond, 1976

There were no press releases or commercials. No advance word whatsoever. When the press corps arrived before the start of the pre-telecast ceremonies at 1980's Grammy Awards at the Shrine Auditorium in Los Angeles, we saw Neil Diamond dueting with Barbra Streisand on the backstage television monitors. Wait a minute! What tape was this?

It wasn't. It was an eleventh-hour rehearsal for a late addition to the Grammy telecast. The famous duo wasn't even introduced as they took the stage to sing that night to a startled and delighted audience. The next morning, America wasn't buzzing about Billy Joel winning album of the year or the Doobie Brothers taking record of the year. They were talking about Barbra and Neil making memorable magic.

But the Grammys would not be Diamond's gem of the year. For a few years, he'd been talking about making a movie. A treatment was done for translating *Beautiful Noise* to the big screen, then there were discussions about *The Gospel Singer* based on Harry Crews' novel (think "Brother Love"), and finally an agent suggested a modern-day remake of the 1927 Al Jolson classic *The Jazz Singer,* one of Hollywood's first talkies.

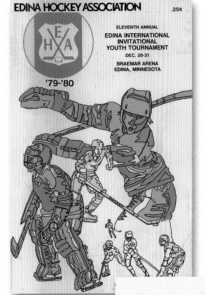

Ad in a 1979–1980 Edina, Minnesota, Youth Hockey Association tournament program. At the time, Neil's merchandise manager, Tom Collins, had a son in the Edina hockey program, so Neil took out a one-page ad. *Courtesy Karen Iffert*

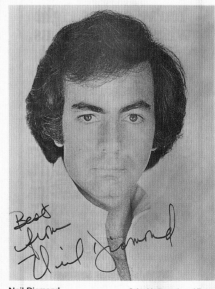

Neil Diamond   Columbia Records and Tapes

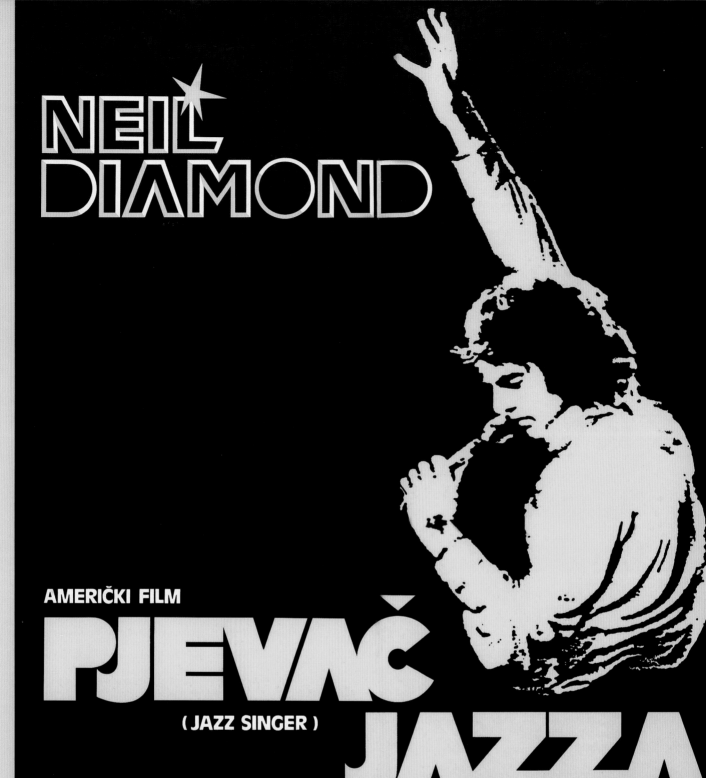

NEIL DIAMOND

AMERIČKI FILM

PJEVAČ

(JAZZ SINGER)

JAZZA

LAURENCE OLIVIER · LUCIE ARNAZ · CATLIN ADAMS

Scenarist
Herbert Baker prema romanu Samsona Raphaelsona

Glazba
Neil Diamond

CROATIA FILM

Režiser
RICHARD FLEISCHER

Q: Is it lonely at the top?

A: It can be, without any intention. But I think if you have good friends and good relationships with people, it's less lonely. But it can be lonely at the top. It's also lonely at the bottom, too. Given the choice, I'd prefer the top and be lonely.

—Neil Diamond, 1976

Sidney J. Furie was brought in to direct, not because he was as well known as Neil, but because he'd directed the screen debuts of Michael Caine (*The Ipcress File*) and Diana Ross (*Lady Sings the Blues*). The storyline somewhat mirrored Diamond's own life: A devout New York cantor leaves his Jewish music (and wife) behind for a pop career and the love of a gentile woman. Laurence Olivier was cast as Diamond's dad, and Lucie Arnaz replaced Deborah Raffin as his love interest. This was filmmaking on the rocks. Two months into the shoot, Furie was fired and replaced by Richard Fleischer, who was best known for the film musical *Dr. Doolittle*.

Like the fictional Jess Robin doubting his switch from pulpit to pop, Diamond had self-doubts about his acting while making the movie. Calling himself "a fish out of water," he told author David Wild in 2000, "I'd come home exhausted, just mentally exhausted. . . . After the first few weeks, you know, I didn't think I could handle it." However, with pep talks from Olivier, Dustin Hoffman, and others, he persevered. In the end, Diamond told the *Los Angeles Times* in 1980: "For me, this was the ultimate bar mitzvah."

But bar mitzvahs don't get reviews other than from gushing relatives. Even though the single from the movie, "Love on the Rocks," shot up the charts in October, the film opened to harsh reviews in December. "He never comes alive," Roger Ebert carped on *At the Movies*. Gene Siskel crowed, "He hasn't done anything here; he's just played Neil Diamond." While the film bombed and pulled in $14 million on its initial run, the soundtrack sold more than four million copies in the United States alone on the strength of three huge hits: "Hello Again," "America," and "Love on the Rocks."

continued on page 89

The Jazz Singer, Japanese import LP.

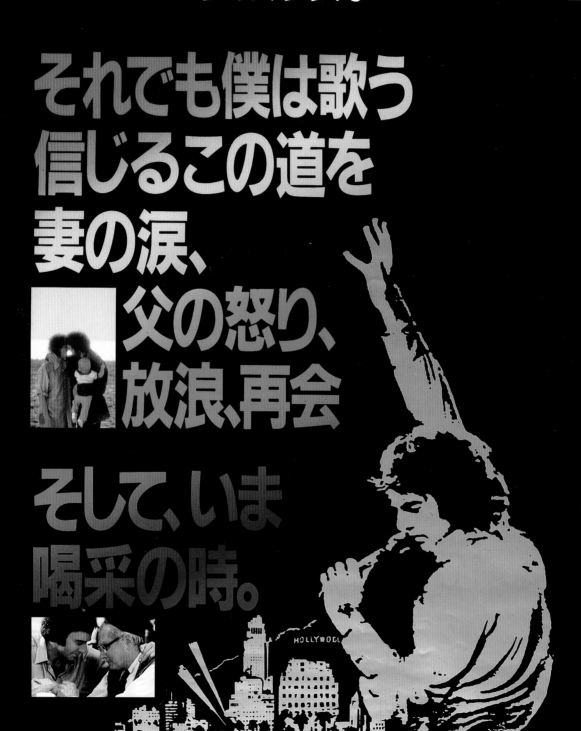

THE JAZZ SINGER

ジャズ・シンガー

挿入歌14曲／自由の国アメリカ／アドン・オラム／おおベイビー／ラブ・オンザ・ロック／ヘイ・ルイーズ
明日のパラダイス／誇り高きロバート・E・リー／サマー・ラブ／ハロー・アゲイン／アカプルコの青い海
人生の詩／エルサレムへの道／コル・ニドレイ／わが名はヤッセル／オリジナルサントラ盤（東芝EMI）

ニール・ダイアモンド主演／ローレンス・オリビエ／ルーシー・アーナス
監督リチャード・フライシャー／製作ジェリー・ライダー／カラー作品
原作本・ヘラルド出版刊／アメリカEMI作品／日本ヘラルド映画

それでも僕は歌う
信じるこの道を
妻の涙、
父の怒り、
放浪、再会

そして、いま
喝采の時。

NEIL DIAMOND
IN STEREO VIDEO

THE JAZZ SINGER

Neil Diamond and his music. Making his motion picture debut, Diamond sings his own chart-topping hits "America," "Love On The Rocks," "Hello Again," plus many more. The original sound track album has already sold more than 7 million units. Now we've brought THE JAZZ SINGER to home video in Stereo on Laserdiscs and selected videocassettes. From Paramount Home Video, of course.

HOME VIDEO

Photo by Michael Ochs Archives/Getty Images

continued from page 85

"Love on the Rocks" started out with a dummy lyric, "scotch on the rocks," based on co-writer Gilbert Bécaud's favorite drink. "America" was "the story of my grandparents," Diamond told the *Los Angeles Times* in 1992. "It's my gift to them, and it's very real for me. Maybe that's why it became so popular. It wasn't thought out or intellectualized, just sheer emotion. In a way, it speaks to the immigrant in all of us. That's what makes it so easy to empathize with the song."

With *The Jazz Singer* LP enriching the coffers of Capitol Records (the film was backed by EMI, the label's parent company), Columbia Records rewarded the pop singer with a new $30 million, eight-album contract. He responded in 1981 with the somewhat lackluster *On the Way to the Sky*, featuring "Yesterday's

Songs," written because "I guess I doubted that any of my early songs would be remembered," as he put it in *In My Lifetime*. (Oy vey, that self-doubt again.)

But whether it's a hit or not, a songwriter keeps crafting songs. After seeing a screening of *E.T.* with the husband-and-wife songwriting team of Burt Bacharach and Carole Bayer Sager, Diamond went back to their apartment and the threesome wrote "Heartlight," which was "a simple musical statement that we all felt sincerely," according to *In My Lifetime*. The song became the title track of Neil's 1982 album, which included six songs co-written by Neil, Bacharach, and Sager.

continued on page 95

I went through some psychological therapy for about three years. It was fascinating for me. It taught me how to verbalize things. To talk, to be able to express myself without holding back, without clamming up, without building up walls around myself, without being self protective. It was really impossible for me to communicate with people on a level other than on a musical level.

—Neil Diamond, 1976

Live at the Forum, June 1983.

Diamond
FORUM CLUB
AFTER SHOW
JUNE 15th
WEDNESDAY

NEIL DIAMOND
AT THE
FORUM

JUNE 13th, 1983   LOS ANGELES, CA
JUNE 14th, 1983   LOS ANGELES, CA
JUNE 15th, 1983   LOS ANGELES, CA
JUNE 16th, 198   LOS ANGELES, CA
JUNE 1 , 198   LOS ANGELES, CA
    8, 1983   LOS ANGELES, CA
JUNE 19th, 1983   LOS ANGELES, CA

SOLD OUT

Live in Concert

Fan Peggy Mayers captured this image in June 1983 at the L.A. Forum, where she attended all seven shows. On the seventh night her camera jammed. When she had the film developed, she discovered that Neil had been exposed in the picture seven times. The image of Neil in the middle is when he had just come up from below the stage to go into "Jonathan."
Courtesy Peggy Mayers

1983.

Fan photos, ASU Activity Center, Tempe, Arizona, June 7, 1983.

1984.

Fan photos, Frank Erwin Center, Austin, Texas, December 3, 1983.

Chicago Stadium, 1982. This shot was not illuminated by house or stage lights. In the midst of "America," photographer Cindy Shunko Jacobsma captured the instant that a pyrotechnic firework popped, timed to coincide with the word

At home in Los Angeles, May 1984. *Photo by Michael Ochs Archives/Getty Images*

continued from page 89

After giving Diamond a record-setting contract, Columbia was concerned about the modest sales of his last two albums. When he submitted his next project in 1983, the self-produced *Primitive*, the label rejected it. He dug his heels in and countered with a lawsuit but eventually backed off and agreed to work with a producer (Denny Diante), drop some tunes, and add three new ones, including "Turn Around." However, the only Diamond tune that went up the charts that year was "Red, Red Wine," which was reworked into a reggae arrangement by UB40.

Frustrated by the *Primitive* ordeal, Diamond returned to his comfort zone: the road. A concert in England was attended by Princess Diana and Prince Charles. It turned out that the twenty-three-year-old Di was a Diamondhead. "I wanted to see you in 1977,"

she reportedly told the Frog King, who was holding a stuffed Garfield toy for two-year-old Prince William. "But my father wouldn't let me. But now he can't tell me what to do."

Diamond understood the influence a father had on a child. The death of his dad, Kieve, on March 23, 1985, of a heart attack in Florida, brought the No. 1 son off the road in Canada and back to Los Angeles for the funeral. The loss of his father, the man whose female pantomimes had helped inspire his own show-business aspirations, inspired several songs for the next album, tentatively titled *Story of My Life*. But once again radio-conscious Columbia was dissatisfied. All the songs were scrapped save the title track, which ended up on an album titled *Headed for the Future*.

Recording in Los Angeles, May 1984. *Photo by Michael Ochs Archives/Getty Images*

Working with several producers and songwriters, including Stevie Wonder, David Foster, and Maurice White of Earth, Wind & Fire, Diamond delivered his most ambitious project since *Beautiful Noise*. "They were all like gambles for me, just shots in the dark with just talented people that I admire," he told me in 1986. "So in that sense, it was a tremendous stretch for me. More like an education, I'd say.... They all came to the project with who they thought Neil Diamond was. And I think it's interesting in that respect because it's like a vocal portrait of somebody from five different angles. And then what the album ended up as—you never really know 'til it all comes together. I'm very pleased with it. I think I got a chance to sing a few songs that I might not have sung otherwise."

Three weeks after the album was released, Diamond starred in *Hello Again*, his first television special in nine years. Half of the program was Neil in concert, which was always a safe bet. Most of the rest of the program featured television goddess Carol Burnett doing comedy sketches with Diamond, who was not exactly Harvey Korman. In a phone interview with me, he made light of his first foray into comedy: "It was weird because I'm not used to having people laugh in the middle of a presentation. But they were laughing and it was fun. It was new for me. I told Carol that those people are interfering with my flow of comedy with their laughing. She got a big kick out of it. And I had a chance to dance with a choreographer and some wonderful trained dancers. The first day I came

Hello Again television special, May 25, 1986.

in for rehearsal with the dancers, the choreographer gave me a pair of Capezio dance shoes and I just said: 'Put an L on the left one and an R on the right one and I'll try to get it as close as I can.' We had fun doing it. I proved I could dance with an ensemble. I'm not going to go out and change professions and become a dancer. But I can do it."

Diamond didn't change professions. He just hit the road, playing three nights in Chicago, five in Detroit, and a record-setting eight nights at Madison Square Garden—his first shows in New York City in a decade and his first ever at the fabled Manhattan venue. Then he returned to the Greek Theatre in Hollywood for an astonishing fourteen shows and another live album. Except for drummer Ron Tutt and percussionist Vince Charles, Diamond had the same bandmembers with whom he'd recorded live in 1976. Souvenir T-shirts proclaimed: "Another Hot August Night." ✦

Courtesy Tom Collins

Last year was very quiet for me.
My dad passed away at the beginning of last year and it kind of took the wind out of me and I didn't really go out and do any shows for six or seven months. . . . This year I feel like I've got my second wind. I'm doing my interviews and I'm doing my TV special and putting out my new album and going out and touring America and seeing if I can get an "A" like I did in college when I worked for that one term where I really worked at it. That's what the year looks like.

—Neil Diamond, 1986

In the studio with *Headed for the Future* co-producer Maurice White of Earth, Wind & Fire, 1986. *Photo by Echoes/Redferns Collection/Getty Images*

The More I Gave, the Less I Got

6

Q: You seem to be a happier person onstage than the person we're led to believe offstage.

A: No. I'm just as happy offstage but I'm much less extroverted. Although on the way into Dayton on our plane, I forced the entire band to sing "Song Sung Blue" and wave. Other than that, I'm perfectly normal.

—Neil Diamond, 1986

David Foster and Neil Diamond had a long history together, but the singer didn't know it. Foster was hired to play keyboards in Diamond's band in the mid-1970s. "I never saw him once," Foster told me in 2008. "We rehearsed for three months, and the bandleader decided I wasn't right." Foster later played keyboards on three Diamond albums—*Heartlight*, *Primitive*, and *Headed for the Future*—and finally met him when they co-wrote a song for *Future*.

By 1988, Foster was becoming one of pop's most successful producers, garnering Grammys for Lionel Richie's *Can't Slow Down* and Barbra Streisand's *Broadway Album*. Foster produced Diamond's *Best Years of Our Lives*. "Neil is quiet. Quiet shouldn't be confused with dark," Foster said. "When it came down to work, he was 'pull up the shirt sleeves and let's get going.' He would drive out to Malibu every day to my studio and we just worked. We made what I thought was a beautiful album. But the public didn't."

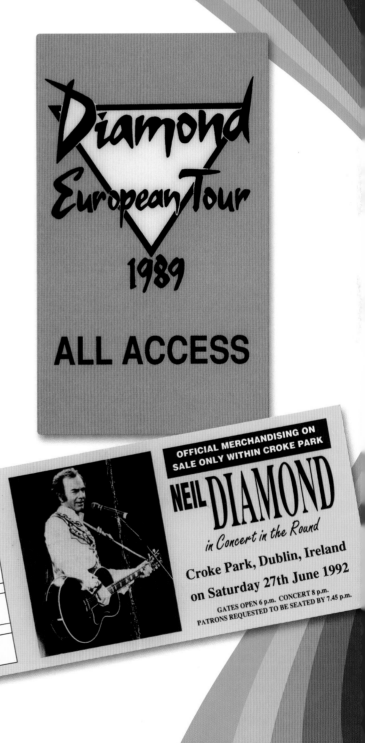

Ahoy, Rotterdam, Holland, November 5, 1989. Photo by Rob Verhorst/Redferns

The album went gold, topping 500,000 in sales, and three tunes, including the title track, showed up on Billboard's adult-contemporary charts. One piece on the album, "Hooked on the Memory of You," had its germination more than a decade earlier. "This was a melody I'd played on piano and taught myself over a period of ten years; sort of a piano lesson for me," Diamond wrote in *In My Lifetime*. "Eventually I completed the melody as a piano piece and realized that it could be more than that. But it was never meant to be a song, just a pretty thing I played on the piano for my own amusement. Eventually it became a song, but that took about fifteen years. It was released as a duet [with Kim Carnes]."

Failing to reach platinum with Foster, Diamond turned to Don Was and Peter Asher. Was, a hot producer he'd never met, had just reinvigorated Bonnie Raitt's career with *Nick of Time* in 1989. Asher, a longtime pal he'd never worked with, was known for producing Linda Ronstadt and James Taylor. (Asher was half of the 1960s duo Peter and Gordon of "World without Love" fame.) Also invited to the party was commercial songwriter extraordinaire Diane Warren, then known for Starship's "Nothing's Gonna Stop Us Now," Cher's "If I Could Turn Back Time," and Milli Vanilli's "Blame It on the Rain." Neil and I discussed this period during a 1992 interview:

Q: Does Columbia put pressure on you to work with hot properties like Diane Warren and Don Was?

A: They never pressured me to do anything. They're allowed to make any suggestion they want, and I tell them that. That was one of their suggestions, and I thought it was a good one. But there's no pressure.

Q: Why did Columbia suggest those two people?

A: They're looking for commercial records from me. And these are commercial writers, and it's what CBS understands. So you give a little to get a lot.

Q: You've generally been receptive to working with other producers.

A: Oh yeah. I'd rather have another producer do it, but sometimes it takes longer to get someone else to do it. So I just do it myself. I have my own studio, I have my own band. It's very easy for me to work

Q: What motivates you?

A: Lot of things. Fear. Boredom. Success. Um, I could probably name a few more if I had to. Excitement.

—Neil Diamond, 1986

a song and rehearse and practice it and record it with my band without having to ask anyone else. It's a tremendous amount of work. The writing is all consuming, and I'd rather concentrate on that. Therefore, if I find a producer I like, I'll ask them to help me.

Despite all the best-laid plans, *Lovescape*, released in 1991, didn't fare much better than *Best Years of Our Lives*, which took three years to go gold. Still, despite relatively soft record sales, Diamond packed every concert hall he played in. His Love in the Round Tour was the second-highest-grossing trek of 1992. That was a remarkable accomplishment considering the economic recession. "I'm lucky," he told me then. "I have an extraordinary audience."

Q: Do audience members need this Neil Diamond fix?

A: Neil Diamond fix, huh? You better ask them about that. I know I need an audience fix every once in a while. That's why I go out, to be reassured by my people that they still remember me and that they haven't all thrown away my CDs in favor of Harry Connick, Jr.

Singing the "Star-Spangled Banner" in one minute flat at Super Bowl XXI, Pasadena, California, January 25, 1987. *Photo by George Rose/Getty Images*

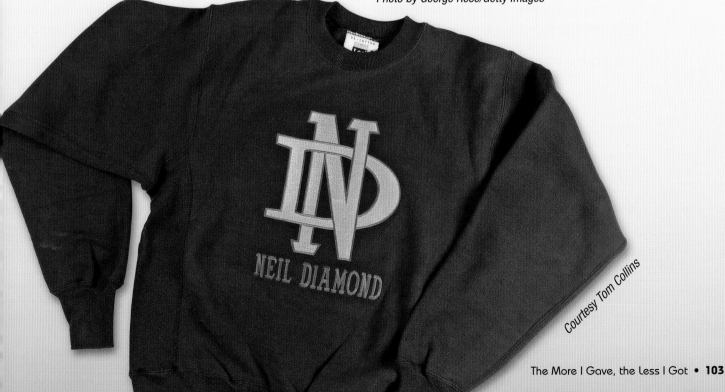

Courtesy Tom Collins

Q: How often do you need that fix? You seem to go on tour every three years.

A: The way it's been working is I've been touring and doing shows and then we'd stop for a while, and I'd start writing and then make an album. And then when the album is done, we'd start preparations to do a show again. It seems to work real nice like that. By the time I've spent fifteen months in a studio with an album, I can't wait to go out. And after two years on the road, I can't wait to get back home and work on some of these ideas and songs I've started and see my family again, get them to know what I look like. There's a lot of give and take, but this seems to work for me. I'm thrilled about being able to go on the road, and just the fact that the new stage is totally fun and—look at that—we're doing great business out there! Go figure it, you know.

Q: You and Bruce Springsteen are the two guys who play arenas who never leave your audiences wanting more. Bruce always says, "I perform every show like it's my last show because it might be." Do you go out there with that attitude?

A: My attitude is a little different, although it's the same thing. I go out realizing that this is something very temporary in my life and that I should be very thankful to have this kind of audience and to be in this kind of situation and therefore I give everything I possibly can every time out. I used to think for many years that each show was my last show, that I would literally die after each show. But a couple years of analysis have talked me out of that.

Q: Why did they convince you that wasn't the case?

A: Because it wasn't the case. I was making it up in my mind. I was scaring myself. I make sure I give everything because I realize that I'm in a special circumstance and I have to handle that very delicately and make sure what's given to me is given back as much as possible as I'm capable of doing it. And that's what it's about.

United Kingdom, circa 1987. Photo by Pete Cronin/Redferns Collection/Getty Images

Near the end of 1992, Diamond decided to go with some proven material and released *The Christmas Album*, accompanied by an HBO special. Clearly, his Jewish background didn't get in the way as his holiday effort climbed to No. 8, giving him his first Top 10 album in ten years. That rebound on the charts convinced Columbia to give him a new contract in 1993 for six more recordings. Immediately, he turned to tried-and-true tunes on *Up on the Roof: Songs of the Brill Building*, celebrating his 1960s New York roots with "Spanish Harlem," "Will You Still Love Me Tomorrow," and "You've Lost That Lovin' Feelin'," a duet with Dolly Parton.

Even though Diamond had renewed his contract with Columbia, 1994 did not turn out to be an artistically fruitful year. He offered yet another concert album, *Live in America*, and *The Christmas Album Vol. 2*, a sequel that not only failed to reach the Top 10 but peaked at No. 51. However, Diamond's name was beginning to sparkle in hipster circles thanks to his song, "Girl, You'll Be a Woman Soon," featured in the Quentin Tarantino film, *Pulp Fiction*. The song, delivered in a faithful rendition by the ultra-cool alt-rock group Urge Overkill, introduced Diamond to a new generation of young music fans. And he appreciated not only the recording but also how the song complemented the scene of an early encounter between soon-to-be-star-crossed lovers John Travolta and Uma Thurman.

"I thought it was dark and dirty and much less naïve and innocent than my original version, which I wrote and recorded when I was twenty-five or twenty-six," Diamond told me in 1996. "I guess it was just moodier than my version. I thought it was perfect. It fit the scene very well."

While that new cachet might have been cool, the downer for Diamond came in October 1994 when Marcia filed for divorce as their twenty-fifth anniversary approached. The dissolution would cost Diamond a staggering $150 million, the biggest celebrity settlement at that time. "I think I'm a very difficult person to be with and to live with," Diamond was quoted by David Wild in *He Is . . . I Say*. "I don't know how these amazing women that I was married to were able to do it." ✦

Courtesy Tom Collins

Q: What kind of workouts do you do?

A: On show days, I do forty minutes of workout in the afternoon—sit-ups, push-ups, stretching, a whole variation of exercises that a trainer worked out for me. And then I do stretching for about forty minutes before the show.

Q: What do you do on the non-show days?

A: I try and hide from the trainer.

—Neil Diamond, 1999

San Jose Arena, San Jose, California, December 11, 1993. *Photo by Tim Mosenfelder/Getty Images*

In 1991, longtime merchandise manager Tom Collins commissioned and presented to Neil the painting that later appeared on this 1992 backstage pass. Neil's cheeky handwritten thank you to Tom acknowledges his fiftieth birthday, which had passed a few months prior. *Courtesy Tom Collins*

92

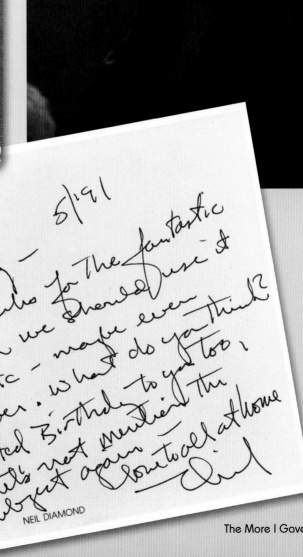

5/'91

Dear Tommy —

Thanks for the fantastic gift! I think we should use it on Tee shirts etc — maybe even program book cover. What do you think?

Happy Belated Birthday to you too, now let's not mention this subject again —

Love to all at home

Neil

NEIL DIAMOND

Bein' Lonesome Enough to Cry

7

The hardest part about it is that people expect some kind of superhero things from you and they don't really understand that you are a person just like they are. You have fears and insecurities and passionate moments and anger and overwork and frustration just like everyone else. But somehow the image of the performer and the celebrity is you get to thinking these people are like gods. And I assure you there are no gods that I've ever met. Just a lot of people trying to get through and, if they're musicians or singer-songwriters, they're trying to do their thing, the thing that they believe they were put on the planet for.

—Neil Diamond, 1992

After his divorce, Diamond rented a house in Nashville. He didn't even tell Columbia Records about his idea. He just wanted to find his songwriting groove again.

"I was just four or five months out of my marriage, and I needed something to throw myself into," he told the *Los Angeles Times* in 1996. "I had no idea whether it was a good idea or bad idea commercially. But I've always thought of Nashville as this special place for writers, and I wanted to get in touch with my writing again. I started a number of songs over the last few years but I finished very few of them because I had no real target. What happened was you'd start a song and maybe get the melody and a verse and a chorus, but then put it down for a while, thinking you'd finish it when it was needed or when you had the energy or the mind for it. And the truth is, I just didn't have the desire for a few years to finish the songs."

continued on page 114

NEIL DIAMOND
Tennessee Moon

HIS NEW ALBUM

18 BRAND NEW SONGS THAT ALREADY SOUND LIKE CLASSICS

ON TOUR
MAY **11** MANCHESTER - NYNEX ARENA
14 NEWCASTLE - ARENA • **21/22** BIRMINGHAM - NEC
25/26 LONDON - WEMBLEY ARENA
JUNE **3** SHEFFIELD - ARENA

COLUMBIA

U.K. promo poster, 1996.

NEC Arena, Birmingham, England, April 3, 1999.
Photo by Peter Still/Redferns

continued from page 111

Diamond met with a group of the top songwriters in country music and invited them, one by one, to sit around the house and make music. "For the most part, the songs were written at the kitchen table, overlooking a pasture in the back," Neil told me in 1996. "One of the writers loaned me some of his horses and we put them out in the pasture; it was a beautiful thing to look out there. We turned on a digital portable tape player and just recorded our work for an hour or two hours.

"I honestly didn't know too much about what country [music] was doing at this time," he continued. "It harked back to my time in Tin Pan Alley, when you worked with people between three and five in the afternoon, when you tried to cut a demo and sell a song and so on."

The veteran songwriter from the East and West Coasts met with Nashville stalwarts Harlan Howard and Dennis Morgan, and newer names Gretchen Peters and Beth Nielsen Chapman. He even penned a tune, "Everybody," with a new writer from Los Angeles, Jesse Diamond, his older son. "Neither one of us could have written the song without the other," Neil said in *In My Lifetime*. "I'd write with Jesse again anytime."

While talking with tunesmith Tom Shapiro, Diamond said he'd always wanted to write a song that was a marriage proposal, so they crafted "Marry Me." With Peters, Diamond compiled "a laundry list of terrible things that could happen to somebody." It turned into "Talking Optimist Blues," which is "one of the silliest songs, and yet one of the more serious songs at the same time."

Diamond did not want this project to turn into his version of Bob Dylan's classic divorce album, *Blood on the Tracks*. "I didn't want this album to be only about my marriage," he explained to the *Los Angeles Times*. "It was only part of my life, certainly an important part . . . and it left a big dent and some bruises, but that's not what this album is about. To me, it is about finding myself as a writer again, experiencing the joy as a writer I haven't had in a long time. I wanted the album to be about the whole person . . . the insanity of the life, the promises you make to yourself, your dreams, your guilt."

Unlike many country writers who've maintained they write better stuff when they're down or heartbroken, Diamond doesn't find depression to be a muse. "I don't like being down and sad and unhappy. It's not an inspiration for me to do any work," he explained to me in 1996. "But the work itself can make me happy. I find if I throw myself into that, then I can at least feel productive in some way or other. It kind of lifted me out of any kind of blue period I might be in. That's exactly what this album did. It lifted my whole life up a few notches. I guess it was good therapy for me then."

Does that mean he's happy now? "It means that I'm still surviving and still productive as a human being and still able to maintain relationships and feel optimistic about the future. Hope is a cuddly thing. It keeps you warm at night."

The reception this project, the eighteen-song *Tennessee Moon*, received was certainly heartwarming. Diamond experienced his most enthusiastic reviews since *Beautiful Noise* in 1976, and, more importantly, the album sold enough copies to land at No. 3 on Billboard's country chart and No. 14 on Billboard's Hot 200. Of course, it didn't hurt that the pop star was joined by country legends Waylon Jennings and Chet Atkins and established singers Hal Ketchum and Raul Malo of the Mavericks. Diamond even made a video for "One Good Love" with Jennings, his buddy of twenty years. To help bridge the gap between pop and country, Neil included a new version of his classic, "Kentucky Woman."

Debuting specially commissioned NYU school song, "Forever NYU," at the school's 170th commencement ceremony, Washington Square Park, New York City, May 16, 2002. *AP Photo/Tina Fineberg*

Q: Bruce [Springsteen] always says "I perform every show like it's my last show because it might be." Do you go out there with that attitude?

A: My attitude is a little different, although it's the same thing. I go out realizing that this is something very temporary in my life and that I should be very thankful to have this kind of audience and to be in this kind of situation and therefore I give everything I possibly can every time out.

—Neil Diamond, 1992

NBC's *Today Show* Summer Concert Series, Rockefeller Plaza, New York City, July 27, 2001. *AP Photo/Richard Drew*

To trumpet his ambitious Nashville project, Diamond filmed a television special, *Neil Diamond: Under a Tennessee Moon*, at the Ryman Auditorium, the mothership of the Grand Ole Opry. Jennings, Atkins, Malo, Ketchum, and budding superstar Tim McGraw appeared on the program.

Diamond, who had already gone through six managers, didn't need a new business guru to explain his place in the grunge era. He knew the score in 1996. "I don't fit into a radio format in the same way that I did in the sixties, seventies, and early eighties. But I'm adapting, not necessarily musically but how this music is promoted. . . . Life holds all kinds of new and exciting vistas. Just call me Neil Bob."

Actually, it was Hollywood that came calling on Neil Bob. "Sweet Caroline" was used in the Matt Dillon/Uma Thurman movie *Beautiful Girls* (is there something about Uma movies and Neil songs?); the Al Pacino/Johnny Depp vehicle *Donnie Brasco* served up "Love on the Rocks."

In 1996, Diamond opened his archives for *In My Lifetime*, a three-disc, seventy-one-song collection of hits from Bang, Uni, and Columbia, as well as demos, rarities, and unreleased recordings, with commentaries by the artist. Two things set this collection apart from most other boxed-set retrospectives: This one landed on the album charts at No. 122, and it went gold.

Since the movies were starting to use his songs, Diamond figured turnabout is fair play. He recorded *The Movie Album: As Time Goes By*, a two-disc set featuring a full orchestra that included film classics like "Moon River," "When You Wish Upon a Star," and "Puttin' on the Ritz." Then it was time to put on another show. By the end of the 1998–1999 tour, *Amusement Business* magazine declared Diamond the top solo touring artist of the 1990s. Not bad for a singer who didn't have one Top 10 hit in the entire decade.

The film world's obsession with Diamond continued in 2001. Smash Mouth, a California rock band, recorded a version of "I'm a Believer" for the soundtrack to the animated sensation *Shrek*. Like the movie, the song went to No. 1. Diamond later reciprocated by writing "You Are My Number One" for Smash Mouth's ensuing album.

The enduring superstar and his music played an even bigger role in the 2001 madcap comedy *Saving Silverman* about a Neil tribute band called Diamonds in the Rough and how the manipulative girlfriend of one of the three lifelong Neil-loving guys forces him to quit the band and burn all his Diamond discs. Diamond not only made a cameo as himself alongside Jack Black, Steve Zahn, Jason Biggs, and Amanda Peet, but he offered a couple of new songs for the movie. Director Dennis Dugan chose "I Believe in Happy Endings" to accompany the closing credits.

"I started writing and I completed the first song," Diamond told Detroit journalist Gary Graff in 2001. "Then I decided to write another one just to give the director a choice. . . . After I finished those two, I was very edgy for some reason, and I realized I had opened up this faucet inside me, this creative faucet, and I wasn't able to close it off. I just continued to write, and one thing led to another, to another, and before I knew it, I had the making of an album."

It wasn't just any album. *Three Chord Opera* marked the first time that Diamond had written an entire project by himself since *Serenade* in 1974. Moreover, it was essentially his first studio album of original music since *Lovescape* in 1991. Fans responded, as *Opera* opened at No. 5, the highest first-week showing in Diamond's career to date. One of the tunes, "Elijah's Song," was a tribute to his newborn grandchild, by Jesse and his actress wife, Sheryl Lee.

Per usual, with a new album, Diamond booked an extensive tour: 120 concerts in 90 cities for 2001–2002. But the real world intervened with the terrorist attacks on New York City and Washington, D.C., on September 11, 2001. Diamond, like the rest of America, would not be detoured. In fact, at every show that fall, "America" became a rousing anthem that resonated with renewed patriotic fervor.

At the world premiere of *Saving Silverman* with the movie's costar, Amanda Peet, February 7, 2001. *Paul Smith/Featureflash/Retna*

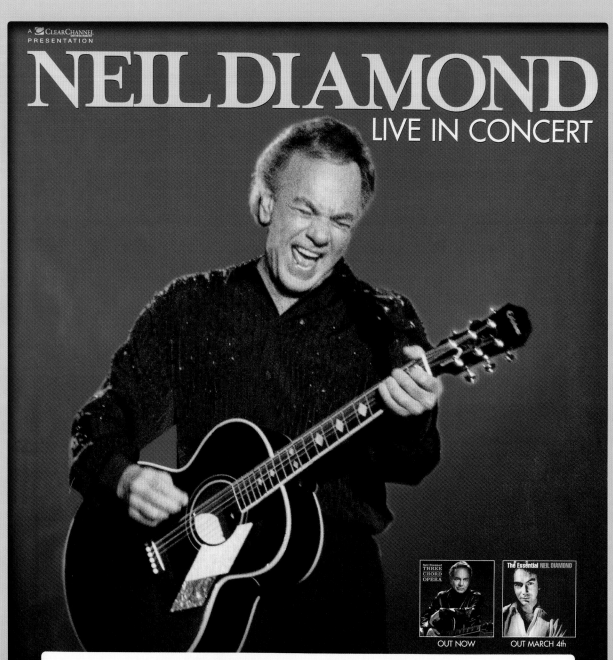

U.K. subway poster, 2002.

BBC TV's *Top of the Pops*, June 27, 2002. *Photo by Mark Allan/WireImage*

Glasgow, Scotland, July 2002. *Photo by Ross Gilmore/Redferns Collection/Getty Images*

"It was a spine-tingling experience," Diamond reflected in a 2005 interview. "The country was ready to get away from their television sets and all the news reports. So we went out on tour ten days after 9/11. We played New York. I had no idea if anybody would show up. Everybody showed up. It was a great, great experience for me. On a spiritual level, it was an important experience for us. It was more than entertainment and fun. We went out and we felt that we had to make a contribution at that point. Everyone in our organization extended themselves. We left a mark and we'll never forget it because we felt we were actually able to do something that was real to us. And it was a good feeling."

He said he's never had that kind of feeling on tour before. "We talk about it all the time because it was something we had not experienced and we're all glad that we did it." ✦

I love [impersonators]

. . . because in a sense they keep the music alive,
and in a way it's flattering, and in a way you have to have
a sense of humor about it.

—Neil Diamond, *Vanity Fair*, February 2001

The Regency Hotel, New York City, November 9, 2005. *AP Photo/Jim Cooper*

Hell Yeah

8

He's like Songwriting 101. There's great chords, great melodies. There's always a lot of passion in his lyrics. Then when he sings it, he delivers everything with so much passion. Neil is amazing.

—**Jimmy Jam, Grammy-winning producer/ songwriter of sixteen No. 1 singles**

It is a hot July night in Madison, Wisconsin, home of the University of Wisconsin, the No. 1 party campus in America, even in the summer. The Alliant Energy Center Memorial Coliseum is packed.

The three college guys behind me keep bellowing "NEIIIIILL!" as if they are watching Neil Young, not Neil Diamond.

A twenty-two-year-old woman next to me stands for the entire show and sings along to nearly every song.

A twenty-year-old shaved-head dude is wearing a hand-lettered T-shirt: "And on the eighth day, God created Neil."

I had to ask these rabid students at the second stop on Neil's 2005 tour: Now that he is working with Rick Rubin—the producer behind Johnny Cash's comeback and hits by the Beastie Boys, the Red Hot Chili Peppers, Jay-Z, Run-DMC, and others—is Neil Diamond becoming hip?

"Whoa!" was the universal reaction to the news. But Sarah Labbus, a recent college grad, had the best answer. "He's Neil Diamond. He doesn't need to be hip," she said, rolling her eyes.

continued on page 126

With Rae Farley, Sydney, Australia, March 1, 2005, prior to kicking off a world tour. *AP Photo/Mark Baker*

Australian promo poster, 2005.

HIS MUSIC HAS ALWAYS BEEN A PART OF OUR LIVES

NEILDIAMOND
LIVE

HOTTER THAN EVER **WITH HIS BRAND NEW SHOW**

SUBIACO OVAL SAT 19 MAR 05 ONE NIGHT ONLY
NEIL PERFORMS THE ENTIRE SHOW ~ FULLY RESERVED SEATING
PREMIUM $99.85 GOLD $60.00
BOOK NOW AT TICKETMASTER7.COM OR 1300 135 915

* Please note that tickets may be subject to additional fees and charges

Produced by DC Touring *ticketmaster7*

Q: During "You Don't Bring Me Flowers," I counted thirty-three separate gestures with your left hand before you reached out and joined hands with Linda Press. Is this conscious? Subconscious?

A: I'm trying to portray the song. I'm not conscious at all about my hand gestures, but now you made me conscious and I'm going to start counting. I never thought of it. It's part of my psychology of the moment. I think there will probably be less hand gestures this time, and each one will count for more. But it's interesting. I'll have to mention that to Linda, and we'll talk it over and see what's going on.

—Neil Diamond, 2008

2005.

neil diamond

WORLD TOUR 2005

Wellington, Christchurch, Sydney, Brisbane,
Perth, Melbourne, Adelaide, Sheffield, Manchester,
Hull, Newcastle, Ipswich, Birmingham, London, Woburn,
Glasgow, Dublin, Bristol, Omaha, Madison, Moline,
Chicago, Detroit, Cleveland, Washington DC,
Philadelphia, Boston, New York, Albany, Buffalo,
Pittsburgh, Columbus, Milwaukee, Minneapolis,
Spokane, Portland, Seattle, Vancouver,
San Jose, Fresno, Sacramento, Los Angeles,
Phoenix, San Antonio, Houston, Dallas,
New Orleans, Biloxi, Tampa, Ft. Lauderdale,
Orlando, Jacksonville, Atlanta
and beyond...

These pages: Madison Square Garden, New York City, August 18, 2005. *Rahav Segev/Retna*

continued from page 123

This concert took place before *12 Songs*, the project with Rubin, hit the stores and Internet outlets. In fact, the release of the album was delayed from September to December. But Neil had already hit the road with clear thoughts about the collaboration. For one, the singer doesn't want the Rubin connection to make him hip. "It's liable to destroy my career," Neil told me with a chuckle. "I've never been considered hip before, although I thought I was miles ahead of most of the stuff that was going on. I never catered to that or pandered to that kind of image. I am what I am. I do what I do."

Rubin wasn't concerned about making Diamond hip, either. "I don't know what makes someone hip," he told me via e-mail. "The goal is artist achievement and the best work we can do with no limitation."
A fan of Diamond's 1960s music, Rubin long had wanted to work with him. He put the word

out. Of course, Neil had his own thoughts about collaborating:

Q: What did you think when Rick Rubin first approached you about the project?

A: I didn't think much of it. I heard a few years ago that there were rumblings that Rick wanted to produce me and loved my songs, et cetera. And he was a rap producer, kind of a pioneer in the rap thing, and now he was producing rock things with some alternative bands. I just didn't understand how I fit into that vein, but Bob Dylan's manager, who I know, called me and said, "I know Rick very well and you should talk to him. He has no agenda. He just loves your stuff. You should talk to him." I called and we had a nice chat. We set up a meeting to get together and, uh, we did. We listened to music. We set up another meeting

and we listened to music and we talked, and we set up another meeting and we talked. And we did this for about four or five months, and then it was time for me. We both kind of unspoken agreed to continue working and get to the next stage, which was to have me write songs that Rick liked and he felt were right for me at this point and the kind of thing he wanted to produce. I spent a little over a year writing, six days a week, seven days a week. Sometimes it was pretty intense.

Out of the twenty or twenty-five songs I started, Rick was attracted to sixteen or seventeen that he felt were in the pocket of where he wanted to go. I completed those. We recorded them. It was great. We had some of the greatest musicians around: Mike Campbell, Smokey Hormel, Benmont Tench. Rick in the control room.

Rubin insisted that Diamond play guitar as he sang. The singer resisted, later explaining to me:

He kind of forced me to play guitar, which I did not want to do. And we argued about it almost every single day. But, of course, I did what he wanted because it's his album. It's my album, but you have to let go and let the producer do what he does. And there's no point in having a producer that you respect if you're going to tell them what to do. So he got his way on those things. I ended up playing on every track of the album—playing and singing live. It was a great experience for me because I hadn't done this kind of playing and singing live [in the studio] since "Kentucky Woman" and "Cherry, Cherry." So it was a new experience for me, something that I didn't think would work because I hadn't done it. But [with] some encouragement from the other musicians and from Rick as well, I went ahead, and it did work out beautifully. The performances were very good, I thought, and the general chemistry of the record reflected that. Not that I was doing such a great job playing, but it was there for me. I was playing and performing the song at the same time and somehow it led to some kind of third thing. The chemistry on the tracks was wonderful, and I would do it again like this next time.

The Zen-like Rubin was less verbose on the subject but no less thrilled. "When Neil would play and sing, it changed his relationship to the song," said the producer, a New Yorker who, like Diamond, attended NYU and has lived in Los Angeles for a couple of decades. "One feels more of a sense of authorship. By playing guitar, Neil controls the rhythm and feel of the songs. It also changes the way he sings them and it becomes a more pure musical act.

"The songs are classic Neil Diamond songs," Rubin continued. "Nobody else could have possibly written them. The sound of the album is very personal, intimate, and honest."

Just how personal is "Delirious Love"? Is it about Neil's nearly decade-long relationship with Rachel (Rae) Farley, an Australian who runs his marketing operation? "Maybe. I tend to want to separate myself from the songs, but the reality is they all come from me and they're all about me. Is that about my relationship? Probably some of it is. I'm crazy about my girl in a way that's an insanity to love. That's what I was trying to portray in my song."

In "Hell Yeah," there's a line: "It's all I got before I die." What's that about? "A lot of that has to do with me and my perspective," Diamond explained. "But he's saying 'I'm going to make the most of this life. Do I love it? Hell yeah. Has it been difficult? Hell yeah. Have I made it through? Hell yeah. Can you make it through? You're damn right.' That's basically what it's about."

In the end, Diamond and Rubin had created, the singer says, "one of my best albums. It's basically a

NBC's *Today Show*, Rockefeller Plaza, New York City, November 8, 2005. © *David Atlas/Retna Ltd.*

stripped-down album. It focuses in on the songs and the performance. It's guitar-driven, and it harkens back to my old days of songwriting. It brings back my focus on the songwriting. It's all of those things. . . . Rick had his own vision about this thing, and he wanted it really stripped down and very nuanced and not orchestrated. I just let him do it. . . . And I'm very pleased with the results. I think he did some amazing work. He was an inspiration for everybody."

Rubin countered with strong praise for Diamond. "He may work harder than any artist I've seen before, and is very hard on himself," Rubin told David Wild in *He Is . . . I Say.* "Saying he's driven doesn't come close; maybe devoted would be a good word."

With Brian Wilson on *The Tonight Show with Jay Leno*, November 14, 2005. *Photo by Paul Drinkwater/WireImage*

Neil is sometimes devoted to other things besides his music. While working on *12 Songs* in 2004, he took a break to perform at a fundraiser for Democratic presidential candidate John Kerry. The program featured a usual cast of Hollywood lefties: Billy Crystal, Jamie Foxx, Ben Affleck, Robert DeNiro, Leonardo DiCaprio, Willie Nelson, and Barbra Streisand. While introducing Diamond, Ben Stiller thanked him for being "the man who helped me to get to second base for the first time in my life" while on a date to see *The Jazz Singer* and for being "my personal savior in a very rocky adolescence." To honor Kerry, Diamond did "America," "Forever in Blue Jeans," "Sweet Caroline," and a live rarity, a "You Don't Bring Me Flowers" duet with Barbra.

Kerry lost the election, but Diamond won big the following fall when *12 Songs* was released. Critics raved (*Newsweek* called it, "the best work Diamond has done in 30 years") and Diamondheads responded. The disc debuted at No. 4, his highest spot on the album charts in twenty-five years. While the music was stripped down, Columbia took a high-tech approach to the CD, encoding it with antipiracy software that turned out to be vulnerable to viruses that could infect computers. Lawsuits ensued, the CDs were recalled from the stores, and *12 Songs* was later re-released. However, the damage was done. Rubin told David Wild, "It was heartbreaking. We put two or more years into that album and to see all of that work compromised by a corporate mistake." ✦

A Geezer Can Kick a Little Butt, Too

I warned Mick Jagger. I said, "You'd better talk to your business office because they made a major mistake by booking you on the same month that I'm going out." I don't think he liked that very much. I'm always a little amazed when I see the turnouts, but I'm thrilled. It makes me happy that I spent so much time getting the show together and making that as wonderful as I can.

—Neil Diamond, 2005

There was no need to worry about Columbia Records messing up Diamond's next album. He now had friends in very high places. Rick Rubin had become co-head of Columbia Records and won the Grammy for producer of the year in 2007.

Working with Rubin and the same cast of musicians was easier the second time around for Neil. "Rick is pretty easygoing in the studio. He's pretty *laissez-faire*. And that's the way I liked it, and that's the way the musicians liked it," Diamond told me in 2008. But writing the material for the album, *Home Before Dark*, was much more difficult.

Rae Farley—his lady, as Neil calls her—had a back injury that damaged a disc in her vertebrae. "She was in extreme pain for a year, and the surgery did not really work. If anything, it made it worse. And I never left her side. I was within fifteen feet of her for the entire year that I took writing this album," Diamond told the *Times* of London in 2008. "So I had to overcome my anxiety for her situation and be there to help her and yet write this album."

"I think of him in the same way I think of Paul Simon—more like a behind-the-scenes guy. Their songs don't necessarily feel autobiographical. They're great craftsmen, great songwriters."
—Jakob Dylan

"He's such a huge guy in the landscape. I think of him as a giant. His music is friendly, and it's accessible. He is what he is."
—Kevin Costner

In the end, he was in such distress that he completed the album in his recording studio. "I considered it a test of my character, of my ability to work, of my ability to help her. But I needed to write. It was easily the most difficult album I have had to write."

In an interview with me, Diamond clarified: "As far as the actual writing of the songs themselves, they came pretty easily. But it was getting over the psychological block in my mind that I had to deal with more than anything else."

The circumstances allowed him to dig deeper emotionally in his writing. "I think maybe the situation I was in had something to do with that. But I wasn't aware of that while I was writing. You get involved in your writing and you let the song take you where it wants to take you. And, uh, so this is where it took me. It took me to places that maybe I haven't been to before, but it's always a relief to get these things out. It's a particularly joyful experience when they come out well, and people like them, and you're able to share them. It was a difficult album to write, very difficult. But the outcome was very, very positive and very satisfying."

Some songs, especially the opening "If I Don't See You Again," seem to deal with death. "I've heard that before, and maybe that's true, although I certainly wasn't aware of that when I was writing it," he told me. "To me, I'm still interpreting some of these songs. With songwriting, you let it happen. A lot of it is stream of conscience, a lot of it is subconscious, and literally and intellectually understanding and explaining these things sometimes doesn't come for a while after they've been written and released and you've listened to them for a while and you get to understand what it was all about, which is an interesting process. There were some dark moments, and there were some light moments. Generally, I'd call it one of my best. I hope I don't have to go through that experience again to get my best. I'll try and do it next time without carrying a heavy load beside the writing."

To duet with Diamond on "Another Day (That Time Forgot)," Rubin brought in one new collaborator: Natalie Maines, lead singer of the Dixie Chicks, with whom he'd won a Grammy for producing their 2006 album of the year, *Taking the Long Way*. The songwriter had unexpectedly come up with the duet idea after he "was working with a little cassette player and my girlfriend was singing along with me while I was writing it, which I didn't appreciate, but she was in the background there. When I listened back to it, I thought, 'Yes, this absolutely should have a girl singing there,' because it sounded great, despite the fact that she can't sing a lick."

Maines sings the track with an immense amount of pain in her voice. Said Diamond: "Maybe it was the song, maybe it was the performance. Natalie and I had a lot of fun doing that—just the two of us away from everybody. They were locked out of the studio, in the little control room. I enjoyed the heck out of it."

He was happy about the album but was sad about Rae's condition and her inability to join him on the tour. "She walks but she is in constant pain and it has changed her life," he said. We talked about his state of mind:

Q: On a scale of one to ten, how happy are you these days?

A: [Laughter] On my scale or your scale? I'm always restless. For some reason, I'm a restless kind of guy. When one thing is completed, I'm looking forward to the next thing. I needed something to occupy my mind and my heart and my emotions and my life. I don't like to be floating around. So I'm forming the next big challenge. That always makes me feel good. If my mind is occupied, I tend to focus less on myself and whatever little problems or big problems I happen to be going through. I'm able to focus on the work so I just make sure there's plenty of work to do.

Performing "Pretty Amazing Grace," *American Idol*, Los Angeles, April 30, 2008.
*Photo by R Mickshaw/*American Idol *2008/Getty Images for Fox*

I was pretty alone on [*Home Before Dark*] in the writing process mostly because of the difficulty that Rae was going through. I felt that it was something that I had to handle and overcome by myself. I saw it as a test, and I was very, very focused in on meeting that test and coming up to the challenge. Because the music had to come and I wanted it to be wonderful and uh, so, uh, I wanted to overcome whatever difficulties I could, and I did, but I didn't particularly like having to do it that way.

—Neil Diamond, 2008

NBC's *Today Show* Summer Concert Series, Rockefeller Plaza, New York City, May 2, 2008. © *Anthony Cutajar/Retna Ltd.*

Q: So where does that leave you on the happy scale right now?

A: On the happy scale, one being depressed and ten being delirious, I'd say I'm about eight or eight and a half.

Q: Do you ever get to ten?

A: I'm there a few times but it doesn't last too long. You have a baby born or you finish an album or you hit No. 1. It lasts about a week.

I love Neil Diamond to death. . . . He's had quite the career and still has quite the career. He's still packing 'em in and calling the shots.

—Brenda Lee

Indeed, *Home Before Dark* debuted at No. 1. The project was set up by Diamond's aggressive new manager, Irving Azoff, as was, among other things, an appearance on *American Idol*, America's most-watched television program.

Was the singer surprised to enter the charts at No. 1? "No, I wasn't surprised. I wasn't honestly thinking about it. It seems to be the thing in the uppermost portions of people's minds, especially the record company, and my management company was very focused in on this album being No. 1. Of course, I helped as much I could. But my main focus is to make wonderful albums and to make beautiful music. I feel I was able to accomplish that with this album. So I was satisfied with it. I was very pleased with it from the get-go. Everything was wonderful and thrilling, but it was beside the point, really."

What did surprise him was that it was his first No. 1 album in his career. "Somehow in my mind—I don't know what the opposite of a state of denial was—but I thought for sure I had a No. 1 album somewhere along the way. I thought *Hot August Night* was No. 1, but then I was told it only went to No. 2, so I was crestfallen. It's a nice feeling to be No. 1. It's very nice. I enjoyed every moment of the time that I was No. 1, and I enjoyed the fact that people became aware that it was my first No. 1 and they were a little amazed at that.

"Also I'm told that I'm the oldest performer on the Billboard charts ever to have a No. 1 album, which amazes me. I don't feel that old. I feel very young, but it's nice to feel that in this market that's filled with young people, or seems to be aimed at young people, that an old geezer can come along and knock a few of them off their perches and say, 'Hey, here's for the senior citizens, and we can kick a little butt, too.'"

Not only did Diamond become the oldest performer to score a No. 1 album, in 2008 he also became the oldest male solo performer to headline an arena tour of such magnitude. It was also Neil's first tour in thirty years without Sal Bonafede, his tour manager who died in 2007 at the age of seventy-four. "It was difficult [putting this tour together] because we were close friends, and Sal really put together the routing and the buildings," Diamond told me. "So I missed him a great deal. But I'm with people now who are as experienced and as excited, and there hasn't been a slip between cup and lip. It's worked very, very well. We're trying some new things, and we're just generally having fun with it. But I do miss Sal."

One of those new things is manager Azoff, one of the most powerful forces in the music business.

I was lucky enough to get to do the *Mojo* Awards in London, and Neil Diamond was there so I made a point backstage to walk up to him and shake his hand and introduce my boys to him. I have a very high regard for Neil Diamond, and he's a guy I think is having a lot of fun now.

—John Fogerty

His clients include the Eagles, Christina Aguilera, Jewel, Morrissey, Steely Dan, and three reunited bands: Van Halen, New Kids on the Block, and Guns N' Roses. He was president of MCA Records for seven years in the 1980s before founding his own Giant Records and then returning to management. In October 2008, his Front Line Management was acquired by Ticketmaster, and he was named CEO of that ticket machine. One thing he brought to Diamond was a change in ticket prices. Azoff broke the $100 barrier with the Eagles in 1994. In 2008, he broke it with Diamond, with top tickets jumping from $75 in 2005 to $120 in 2008.

Said Diamond: "It's just the nature of the world. Everything is more expensive. The shows are extraordinarily expensive to do. The productions are expensive to do. I've tried always to keep the ticket prices down. I'm still trying to keep the ticket prices down, and sometimes it catches up with you and you have to pay the bills. That's unfortunately the reality of the world today." In other words, Diamond isn't exactly making more for this tour? "That's exactly right," he said.

Since Diamond didn't do any selections from *12 Songs* on his 2005 tour, he made sure to include a couple on his thirty-seven-city 2008–2009 tour, working up new arrangements to include drums. He also featured five or six songs a night from *Home Before Dark*—the most songs from a brand-new album he's ever done in concert. Just how does he come up with the set list?

"It has to be felt," he explained in a telephone conference with several writers before the start of his 2008 tour. "You have to imagine yourself in that circumstance in front of an audience. That's usually how

it starts with me. What is the first song? From the first song, I know what my last song is going to be, which is 'Brother Love.' All I have to do is fill in the blank spaces for the next two hours, but it's mostly imagining how the audience is going to respond to each song in order. Does it make sense? Does it follow the emotional mountains and valleys that I believe a good set list should contain? Does it leave the audience feeling satiated and uplifted? Does it please you, meaning me? Does it please my band? Because we've been together so long that they will definitely have their say if they feel strongly about something; sometimes I resist it and sometimes I'll go with it. But I think there's a sixth sense somewhere involved in that in how a set list can involve an audience for two hours and keep them enthralled and entertained and having a good time."

Wait a minute. Did he just say that "Brother Love's Traveling Salvation Show" is always his last song? Then what happened on opening night in St. Paul on July 19, 2008, when he didn't end with "Brother Love"?

The following night, July 20 at St. Paul's Xcel Energy Center, Diamond didn't have any of the distractions of the night before. No microphone or sound system malfunctions. He was looser, more relaxed, more animated and active, and in consistently good voice. In other words, he was "on." He looked as if he was having a much more enjoyable time onstage than the previous night. Moreover, the audience seemed more energetic and younger, which always invigorates his performance. And he closed with "Brother Love's Traveling Show," just like he always does. ✦

Neil Diamond

will be around until there's nobody in his audience around . . . . He wants it that bad, he loves it that bad, that he needs performing and feeds off what the public gives back to him. And he takes pride in what he's doing.

—Frankie Valli

This silkscreen poster

by Micah Smith was commissioned by Myspace.com for its Secret Shows pro-gram in which seasoned artists play free shows in small clubs. Neil was asked to play The Bitter End (capacity: 125) in his native New York City on May 7, 2008. He hadn't played the venue in forty years. Smith recalls: "After the show, Myspace relayed Mr. Diamond's gratitude and appreciation of the poster design. A few days later, Mr. Diamond's manager sent a note asking for my street address so he could send me a signed poster. A week or so passed and I received one of my posters in a tube with this scribbled on it:

'To Micah—
What a wonderful poster. I love it!
All my best,
Neil Diamond'"

Friday Night with Jonathan Ross, London, May 23, 2008. *Both Brian J. Ritchie/Rex Features*

U.K. promo poster, 2008.

Glastonbury, England, June 29, 2008. *Photo by Jim Dyson/Getty Images*

Encore

I just want to feel productive, feel as though I'm making some kind of contribution and paying my way for the good fortune that I've had. That's basically it. I want to feel as though I have a value here on this planet. That motivates me. Otherwise, I'm just a slug, hanging on a barnacle. I want to feel as though I can make a contribution. That's what I try for. I'm not motivated by what I've done in the past. It's done and I can enjoy it. That doesn't motivate me for the future. I want to feel as though I still have some kind of meaning in the scheme of it all.

—Neil Diamond, 2008

"Let's start at fifty thousand for a car that sings like Neil Diamond," Jimmy Kimmel proposes to the black-tie crowd. "Neil Diamond lives in the trunk."

Kimmel, that prince of late-night TV, is the emcee/auctioneer for the 2009 MusiCares gala honoring Neil Diamond as Person of the Year for his charitable work. For $1,250 you get a seat at the auction, dinner, and a concert by fourteen stars singing the songs of Neil—from the Jonas Brothers and soon-to-be best new artist Grammy winner Adele to Tim McGraw and grunge hero Chris Cornell of Soundgarden fame.

Kimmel assures the 2,200 music-biz movers and shakers at the Los Angeles Convention Center that he is indeed a Diamond lover: "My kids are named Desiree and Soolaimon." The gala-goers have names like Barry Bonds, John Stamos, Sarah Silverman, Jason Mraz, Ashford & Simpson, Rick Rubin, Irving Azoff, and Marshall Gelfand (Neil's forever accountant, who is certainly better with numbers than he is with public speaking).

These are the kind of people who would buy a new—or used—car from Kimmel. He fetches $55,000 for that 2009 Brooklyn Roads Acura TL, customized with a sound system by a recording engineer from the same Brooklyn neighborhood as Neil. In the 'hood is not exactly Neil in the trunk. But a car that *Neil* used to drive—a 1956 Thunderbird convertible that his band gave him—pulls in $75,000 in tonight's auction. An autographed Eric Clapton guitar commands $40,000. A signed copy of Neil's 1976 *Rolling Stone* cover story goes for $400, while a similarly vintage cover with Paul Simon's John Hancock sells for a mere $275. By the time the online aspect of this auction is over, the event will raise $3.7 million for MusiCares, the charity arm of the Grammy Awards that has given out $15 million in the past five years to struggling members of the music community.

Enough with the accounting. It's time for the "greatest night of karaoke ever," as Kimmel puts it. Those new kids on the block, the Jonas Brothers, are chosen to open the post-dinner concert, with "Forever in Blue Jeans." "Aren't they adorable?" Kimmel insists. "These kids wouldn't even have sideburns if it weren't for Neil Diamond."

Jennifer Hudson, who went from *American Idol* reject to Oscar winner, is adorable and awesome, taking "Holly Holy" to a Southern church with pretty amazing grace. Then it's Kid Rock's turn, going Southern rock on "Thank the Lord for the Night Time." Urge Overkill dusts off "Girl, You'll Be a Woman Soon," which made them famous via the movie *Pulp Fiction*. The 1990s Chicago rockers love Neil. "He's the master of the three-chord song," lead singer Nash Kato acknowledges to Rollingstone.com backstage. "He was our version of punk rock."

The 51st Annual Grammy Awards, Staples Center, Los Angeles, February 8, 2009. *Photo by Jeff Kravitz/FilmMagic*

I'm a huge fan of Neil Diamond's, and I love his recent records with Rick Rubin. I saw him at Glastonbury as well, which was great. I kind of see him as a bit of a crooner, which I love and I find that so glamorous. And I do love his voice.

—Adele

Coldplay, the hottest rock band of the moment, goes unplugged with an acoustic rockabilly reading of "I'm a Believer" that suggests the Everly Brothers as a quartet. Raul Malo, who recorded with Diamond on "Tennessee Moon," brings Roy Orbison–like loneliness to "Solitary Man." Jazz stylist Cassandra Wilson mesmerizes with a penetrating reinvention of "September Morn," featuring trumpeter Terence Blanchard's expressive solo. Foo Fighters transform "Delirious Love" into a rip-roaring rocker, while Josh Groban follows by crooning an elegant "Play Me" at the piano. These stars have put too much into their performances to dismiss this as great karaoke.

The house band for the night adds considerable luster: Tom Petty keyboardist Benmont Tench (who played on Neil's *12 Songs* and *Home Before Dark*),

bassist/bandleader Don Was (who produced Neil's *Lovescape*), and legendary drummer Jim Keltner (CSNY, John Lennon, George Harrison, Ringo Starr, Bob Dylan, Traveling Wilburys). Some of tonight's performers are self-contained groups, including one introduced by Diamond himself via video. The story begins with him phoning Eddie Vedder of Pearl Jam to ask him to play at the charity gala, but he has mistakenly dialed a different Eddie—Eddie Rodriguez. Delivering this tale with all the deadpan of Woody Allen, Neil learns that this Eddie has a band, and so why not? Neil invites them to the MusiCares affair. Without even a mention of the group's name, Eddie Rodriguez and Los Volcanes appear live and serve up a tasty Tejano mix of "Red, Red Wine."

MusiCares Person of the Year tribute, Los Angeles, February 6, 2009. *AP Photo/Matt Sayles*

He's the Jewish Elvis—I don't think you can sum it up any better than that. He's just kind of his own thing; he found his niche and he stuck with it. Not only has his music remained timeless, but he kind of has, too, which is very rare.

—**Kid Rock**

Rustic Bread Basket

An assortment of rustic Breads, Crisps, and Rolls
served with sun-dried Tomato Butter, Pesto Butter, Sweet Cream Butter,
Three-olive Tapenade, Olive Oil, and Aged Balsamic Vinegar

Salad

Mission Figs, marinated Artichokes and braised Fennel with
organic Baby Greens, fresh Orange and Grapefruit supremes,
and Candied Pecans ~ Sweet Apricot-Orange Vinaigrette

Entrée Combination

Pine Valley Farms boneless Beef Short Rib braised with a blend of organic
Beech, Oyster, and Crimini Mushrooms ~ HALL Cabernet Sauce, Napa
served with pan-roasted free-range Chicken
and an assortment of local, organic, and sustainable Baby Vegetables

Dessert

"Sweet Caroline" Medley:

"Red Red Wine" Spiced Poached Sickle Pear with Dried Fruit
Petite Almond Florentine filled with White Chocolate Grand Marnier Mousse,
"Crunchy Granola Suite" and California Berries
"Cherry Cherry" Chocolate Truffle Lollipop

MusiCares and The Los Angeles Convention Center are proud to support
regional growers and sustainable, organic farming.

Weiser Family Farm, Tehachapi ~ Underwood Ranch, Oxnard ~ Rising C Ranch, Reedley
See Canyon Ranch, San Luis Obispo ~ Pine Valley Farm ~ Catania, Fresno
Fresh Origin, San Diego ~ Gourmet Mushrooms, Sebastipol ~ Driscoll Farms

MusiCares

Rick Wineman, *Executive Chef*

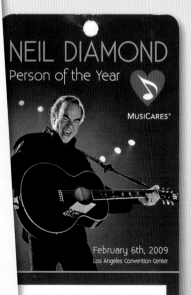

NEIL DIAMOND
Person of the Year

MusiCares

February 6th, 2009
Los Angeles Convention Center

Table # ___154___

My brother is obsessed with Neil Diamond. He's sixteen. He walks around the house with his portable iPod player on his shoulder and blasts Neil Diamond songs all throughout the house.

—Taylor Swift

If Eddie or any of the other singers isn't certain of the lyrics, there is a huge screen at the back of the ballroom broadcasting the words in three-foot-high letters. No teleprompters are needed for the man of the moment. Neil takes the stage, accepts his trophy, and runs through a list of thank yous—his children, grandchildren, and mother, Rose, all of whom are in the audience. He reminisces about what prompted him to learn how to play guitar. "The Brooklyn Dodgers had left Brooklyn and I was in a state of depression," he says. "So I decided to take music lessons because I was really down." His parents paid off the guitar—$1 a week for ten weeks. "So it was a good investment, Mom," he continues. "You invested $10 and you made a life for me. I thank you for that, Mom."

He thanks Columbia Records, his label of thirty-four years. "We're still not tired of each other," he says. "They still want to re-sign me. I'm going to send them to Irving Azoff and see what Irving thinks about it. [The crowd chuckles.] Good luck, Columbia Records."

Not only does Diamond acknowledge his first music lessons, he flashes back to writing his first song fifty years ago. "I wrote it for a girl I fell in love with. And she liked the song so much she married me," he explains as the audience goes "awww." "I should have realized at that point how dangerous songwriting could be. [The crowd laughs.] I'm careful about who I write songs with nowadays. I try to write using anonymous names."

Performing with Faith Hill, MusiCares Person of the Year tribute, Los Angeles, February 6, 2009. *AP Photo/Matt Sayles*

Without any further ado, Neil strikes up his band. At previous MusiCares affairs saluting the likes of Tony Bennett, Aretha Franklin, Luciano Pavarotti, Bono, Billy Joel, Elton John, Sting, and James Taylor, the honoree typically sang two or three songs as a cameo at the end. However, Neil turns this evening into a mini Diamond concert.

Backed by his touring band, he commands the stage for thirty-five minutes, dishing up six songs, including "Cherry, Cherry" and "You Don't Bring Me Flowers," with surprise guest Faith Hill. This isn't exactly a Diamond crowd. They know him but not new numbers like "Pretty Amazing Grace." However, they stand up for "America," and for the closing "Sweet Caroline," all of them reach out and wave their arms in unison. Neil is hugging Cassandra Wilson with one arm and soul singer Eric Benet with the other, as the all-star cast joins him onstage, singing "So good, so good, so good."

"Thank you for having such big hearts. We love you for it," Neil assures the gala-goers as the band plays on. "Thank you for putting your dough where your mouth is. We'll see you again, OK? Alright band, take us out. . . ." ◆

The Neil Diamond event was awesome. We were a little nervous about whether we were going to be able to do it. . . . Meeting Neil Diamond—that guy is awesome. He's kind of like as classic a character as people perceive him to be. He said really cool things to us. He wrote us all individual letters afterward thanking us for being a part of it. It's very cool to have a letter from Neil Diamond.

—Joe Jonas of the Jonas Brothers

Discography

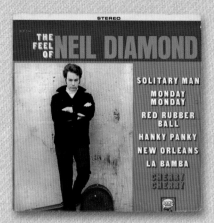

The Feel of Neil Diamond • 1966
Producers: Jeff Barry and Ellie Greenwich
Label: Bang
Songs: Solitary Man; Red Rubber Ball; La Bamba; Do It; Hanky Panky; Monday, Monday; New Orleans; Someday Baby; I Got the Feelin' (Oh No No); I'll Come Running; Love to Love; Cherry, Cherry
Noteworthy: Originally issued in mono, this has never been released on CD.

Just for You • 1967
Producers: Jeff Barry and Ellie Greenwich
Label: Bang
Songs: Girl, You'll Be a Woman Soon; The Long Way Home; Red, Red Wine; You'll Forget; The Boat that I Row; Cherry, Cherry; I'm a Believer; Shilo; You Got to Me; Solitary Man; Thank the Lord for the Night Time
Album peak: No. 80
Singles peak: Cherry, Cherry, No. 6
Noteworthy: This rarity has never been released on CD, but most of the tracks were included on the compilation *Early Classics*.

Velvet Gloves and Spit • 1968
Producers: Tom Catalano, Joe Foster, Andy Morten, Chip Taylor, and Neil Diamond
Label: Uni
Songs: A Modern Day Version of Love; Sunday Sun; Honey-Drippin' Times; The Pot Smoker's Song; Brooklyn Roads; Shilo; Two-Bit Manchild; Holiday Inn Blues; Practically Newborn; Knackelflerg; Merry-Go-Round
Singles peak: Brooklyn Roads, No. 58
Noteworthy: The LP was released in fall 1968 and then reissued, with a new cover and an eleventh song (Shilo), in spring 1969.

Brother Love's Traveling Salvation Show • 1969
Producer: Chips Moman
Label: Uni
Songs: Brother Love's Traveling Salvation Show; Dig In; River Runs, Newgrown Plums; Juliet; Long Gone; And the Grass Won't Pay No Mind; Glory Road; Deep in the Morning; If I Never Knew Your Name; Memphis Streets; You're So Sweet Horseflies Keep Hangin's 'Round Your Face; Hurtin' You Don't Come Easy
Album peak: No. 82
Singles peak: Brother Love's Traveling Salvation Show, No. 22
Noteworthy: Sweet Caroline was added to the second pressing of the album and the title changed to *Sweet Caroline: Brother Love's Traveling Salvation Show*.

Touching You, Touching Me • 1969
Producers: Tom Catalano and Tommy Cogbill
Label: MCA
Songs: Everybody's Talkin'; Mr. Bojangles; Smokey Lady; Holly
Holy; Both Sides Now; And the Singer Sings His Song; Ain't
No Way; New York Boy; Until It's Time for You To Go
Album peak: No. 30
Singles peak: Holly Holy, No. 6
Noteworthy: Diamond's first big seller, this LP had covers
of songs by Joni Mitchell, Jerry Jeff Walker, Fred Neil, and
Buffy Sainte-Marie.

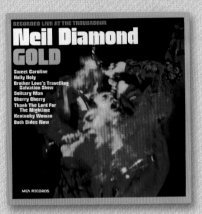

Gold • 1971
Producer: Tom Catalano
Label: Uni
Songs: Lordy; Both Sides Now; Solitary Man; Holly Holy;
Cherry, Cherry; Kentucky Woman; Sweet Caroline; Thank
the Lord for the Night Time; And the Singer Sings His Song;
Brother Love's Traveling Salvation Show
Album Peak: No. 10
Noteworthy: This concert album was recorded with Diamond
and three other musicians (and female backup singers) at
the Troubadour, the hip Hollywood rock club.

Tap Root Manuscript • 1970
Producers: Tom Catalano and Neil Diamond
Label: MCA
Songs: Cracklin' Rosie; Free Life; Coldwater Morning; Done
Too Soon; He Ain't Heavy, He's My Brother; Childsong; I
Am the Lion; Madrigál; Soolaimon; Missa; African Suite;
Childsong (reprise)
Album peak: No. 13
Singles peak: Cracklin' Rosie, No. 1
Noteworthy: One entire side of this LP was devoted to the
"African Trilogy" suite, which included the hit Soolaimon.

Stones • 1971
Producer: Tom Catalano
Label: MCA
Songs: I Am . . . I Said; The Last Thing on My Mind; Husbands
and Wives; Chelsea Morning; Crunchy Granola Suite; Stones;
If You Go Away; Suzanne; I Think It's Gonna Rain Today; I Am
. . . I Said (reprise)
Album peak: No. 11
Singles Peak: I Am . . . I Said, No. 4
Noteworthy: Yes, the album opens and closes with the same
song, though the first version is sixty seconds longer. Plus,
the ace songwriter covered hits by such stellar tunesmiths
as Roger Miller, Randy Newman, Leonard Cohen, and
Joni Mitchell.

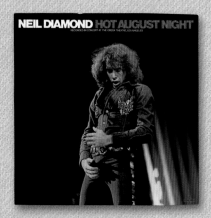

Hot August Night • 1972
Producer: Tom Catalano
Label: MCA
Songs: Prologue; Crunchy Granola Suite; Done Too Soon; (dialogue); Solitary Man; Cherry, Cherry; Sweet Caroline; Porcupine Pie; You're So Sweet; Red, Red Wine; Soggy Pretzels; And the Grass Won't Pay No Mind; Shilo; Girl, You'll Be a Woman Soon; Walk on Water; Kentucky Woman; Stones; Play Me; Canta Libre; Morningside; Song Sung Blue; Cracklin' Rosie; Holly Holy; I Am . . . I Said; Soolaimon/ Brother Love's Traveling Salvation Show
Album Peak: No. 5
Noteworthy: Three songs—Walk on Water, Kentucky Woman, and Stones—were added to this live-at-the-Greek-Theatre album for the 2000 reissue.

Jonathan Livingston Seagull • 1973
Producer: Tom Catalano
Label: Columbia
Songs: Prologue; Be; Flight of the Gull; Dear Father; Skybird; Lonely Looking Sky; The Odyssey: Be/Lonely Looking Sky/ Dear Father; Anthem; Be; Skybird; Dear Father; Be
Album peak: No. 2
Singles peak: Be, No. 34
Noteworthy: Diamond won his first and only Grammy for this album, for best instrumental composition for a movie or television show. The album also snared the Grammy for best spoken-word album, with narration by Richard Harris.

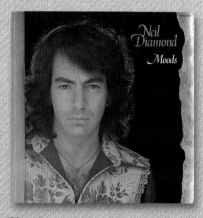

Moods • 1972
Producers: Tom Catalano and Neil Diamond
Label: MCA
Songs: Song Sung Blue; Captain Sunshine; Porcupine Pie; Canta Libre; Morningside; Play Me; Gitchy Goomy; Walk on Water; High Rolling Man
Album peak: No. 5
Singles peak: Song Sung Blue, No. 1
Noteworthy: Diamond didn't think Song Sung Blue should be a single; he preferred Play Me.

Serenade • 1974
Producer: Tom Catalano
Label: Columbia
Songs: Lady Magdalene; The Last Picasso; Yes I Will; I've Been This Way Before; Rosemary's Wine; Longfellow Serenade; Reggae Strut; The Gift of Song
Album peak: No. 3
Singles peak: Longfellow Serenade, No. 5
Noteworthy: Since he was on a sabbatical from touring, Diamond flew to Spain, West Germany, and England to promote the album on television shows.

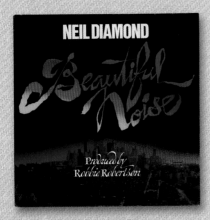

Beautiful Noise • 1976

Producer: Robbie Robertson
Label: Columbia
Songs: Beautiful Noise; Street Life; Home Is a Wounded Heart; Jungletime; Don't Think . . . Feel; Lady-Oh; Dry Your Eyes; Signs; Surviving the Life; Stargazer; If You Know What I Mean
Album peak: No. 4
Singles peak: If You Know What I Mean, No. 11
Noteworthy: Diamond felt so strongly about his collaboration with the hip leader of The Band, Bob Dylan's old backup band, that "Produced by Robbie Robertson" was printed on the front cover.

I'm Glad You're with Me Here Tonight • 1977

Producer: Bob Gaudio
Label: Columbia
Songs: Desirée; Free Man in Paris; God Only Knows; Let the Little Boy Sing; I'm Glad You're Here with Me Tonight; Lament in D Minor/Dance of the Sabres; You Don't Bring Me Flowers; Once in a While; Let Me Take You in My Arms Again; As If
Album peak: No. 6
Singles peak: Desiree, No. 16
Noteworthy: This features covers of huge hits by the Beach Boys and Joni Mitchell, as well as Neil's solo rendition of You Don't Bring Me Flowers.

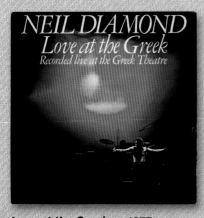

Love at the Greek • 1977

Producer: Robbie Robertson
Label: Columbia
Songs: Streetlife; Kentucky Woman; Sweet Caroline; The Last Picasso; Longfellow Serenade; Beautiful Noise; Lady Oh; Stargazer; If You Know What I Mean; Surviving the Life; Glory Road; Song Sung Blue; Holly Holy; Brother Love's Traveling Salvation Show; Jonathan Livingston Seagull: Be/Dear Father/Lonely Looking Sky/Sanctus/Skybird/Be; I've Been This Way Before
Album peak: No. 8
Noteworthy: Henry Winkler, in the character of the Fonz, joined Diamond for Song Sung Blue on this live album recorded at the Greek Theatre in Hollywood.

You Don't Bring Me Flowers • 1978

Producer: Bob Gaudio
Label: Columbia
Songs: The American Popular Song; Forever in Blue Jeans; Remember Me; You've Got Your Troubles; You Don't Bring Me Flowers; The Dancing Bumble Bee/Bumble Boogie; Mothers and Daughters, Fathers and Sons; Memphis Flyer; Say Maybe; Diamond Girls
Album peak: No. 4
Singles peak: You Don't Bring Me Flowers, No. 1
Noteworthy: The title song wouldn't have happened if Neil hadn't been sitting next to TV producer Norman Lear at George Burns' eightieth birthday party and cheekily asked "What brilliant new show do you have planned that would need an equally brilliant theme song?"

September Morn • 1979

Producer: Bob Gaudio
Label: Columbia
Songs: September Morn; Mama Don't Know; That Kind; Jazz Time; The Good Lord Loves You; Dancing in the Street; The Shelter of Your Arms; I'm a Believer; The Sun Ain't Gonna Shine Anymore; Stagger Lee
Album peak: No. 10
Singles peak: September Morn, No. 17
Noteworthy: Diamond collaborated with Frenchman Gilbert Bécaud on two songs, including the title tune.

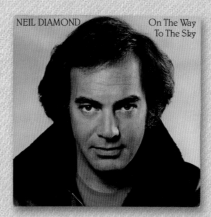

On the Way to the Sky • 1981

Producer: Neil Diamond
Label: Columbia
Songs: Yesterday's Songs; On the Way to the Sky; Right by You; Only You; Save Me; Be Mine Tonight; The Drifter; Fear of the Marketplace; Rainy Day Song; Guitar Heaven; Love Burns
Album peak: No. 17
Singles peak: Yesterday's Songs, No. 11
Noteworthy: The album's final track, Love Burns, was co-written by the two keyboardists in Neil's touring band, Alan Lindgren and Tom Hensley.

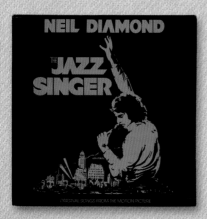

The Jazz Singer • 1980

Producer: Bob Gaudio
Label: Columbia
Songs: Love on the Rocks; Hello Again; America; Songs of Life; Amazed and Confused; Summerlove; Kol Nidre; On the Robert E. Lee; Acapulco; Hey Louise; Jerusalem; You Baby
Album peak: No. 3
Singles peak: Love on the Rocks, No. 2
Noteworthy: While Gilbert Bécaud co-wrote five songs with Neil, the singer teamed with three of his bandmembers on three other songs. Adon Olom and Kol Nidre are Jewish prayers, the latter part of Yom Kippur services.

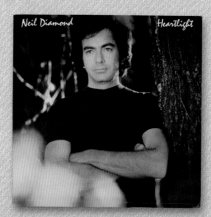

Heartlight • 1982

Producers: Neil Diamond, Burt Bacharach, Carole Bayer Sager, Alan Lindgren, Richard Bennett, and Michael Masser
Label: Columbia
Songs: Heartlight; Lost Among the Stars; Hurricane; I'm Alive; Comin' Home; In Ensenada; A Fool for You; Star Flight; I'm Guilty; Front Page Story; First You Have to Say You Love Me
Album peak: No. 9
Singles peak: Heartlight, No. 5
Noteworthy: Six of the songs were co-written by Neil with the husband-and-wife team of Burt Bacharach and Carole Bayer Sager.

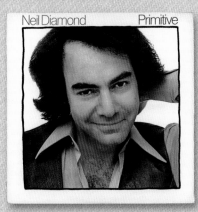

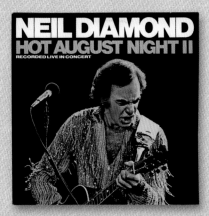

Primitive • 1984
Producers: Neil Diamond, Denny Diante, and Richard Bennett
Label: Columbia
Songs: Turn Around; Primitive; Fire on the Tracks; Brooklyn on a Saturday Night; Sleep with Me Tonight; Crazy; My Time with You; Love's Own Song; It's a Trip (Go to the Moon); You Make It Feel Like Christmas; One by One
Album Peak: No. 35
Singles peak: Turn Around, No. 62
Noteworthy: The label rejected Neil's first self-produced version of this record, he sued, producer Denny Diante was brought in, some tunes were dropped, and three, including Turn Around, were added.

Hot August Night II • 1987
Producer: Val Garay
Label: Columbia
Songs: Song of the Whales (fanfare); Headed for the Future; September Morn; Thank the Lord for the Night Time; Cherry, Cherry; Sweet Caroline; Hello Again; Love on the Rocks; America; Forever in Blue Jeans; You Don't Bring Me Flowers; I Dreamed a Dream; Back in L.A.; Song Sung Blue; Cracklin' Rosie; I Am . . . I Said; Holly Holy; Soolaimon; Brother Love's Traveling Salvation Show; Heartlight
Album peak: No. 59
Noteworthy: Val Garay, Linda Ronstadt's longtime engineer, was brought in as producer.

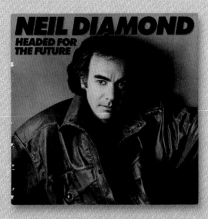

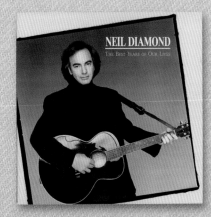

Headed for the Future • 1986
Producers: David Foster, Maurice White, Stevie Wonder, Burt Bacharach, Carole Bayer Sager, Tom Hensley, Alan Lindgren, and Neil Diamond
Label: Columbia
Songs: Story of My Life; It Should Have Been Me; The Man You Need; Lost in Hollywood; Stand Up for Love; I'll See You on the Radio (Laura); Me Beside You; Angel; Love Doesn't Live Here Anymore; Headed for the Future
Album peak: No. 20
Singles peak: Headed for the Future, No. 53
Noteworthy: Working with nine different producers in nine different studios, Diamond collaborated with Stevie Wonder, Bryan Adams, Burt Bacharach, and Maurice White of Earth, Wind & Fire.

The Best Years of Our Lives • 1988
Producer: David Foster
Label: Columbia
Songs: The Best Years of Our Lives; Hard Times for Lovers; This Time; Everything's Gonna Be Fine; Hooked on the Memory of You; Take Care of Me; Baby Can I Hold You; Carmelita's Eyes; Courtin' Disaster; If I Couldn't See You Again; Long Hard Climb
Album peak: No. 46
Noteworthy: Super-producer David Foster, who had played keyboards on three previous Diamond albums, co-wrote four songs with the singer.

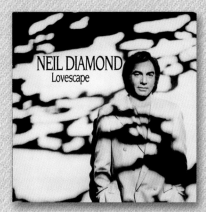

Lovescape • 1991
Producers: Peter Asher and Don Was
Label: Columbia
Songs: If There Were No Dreams; Mountains of Love; Don't Turn Around; Someone Who Believes in You; When You Miss Your Love; Fortune of the Night; One Hand, One Heart; Hooked on the Memory of You; Wish Everything Was Alright; The Way; Sweet L.A. Days; All I Really Need Is You; Lonely Lady #17; I Feel You; Common Ground
Album peak: No. 44
Noteworthy: He performed a duet with Kim Carnes on Hooked on a Memory of You and dusted off One Hand, One Heart from *West Side Story*.

The Christmas Album • 1992
Producer: Peter Asher
Label: Columbia
Songs: O Come, O Come Emmanuel/We Three Kings of Orient Are; Silent Night; Little Drummer Boy; Santa Claus Is Coming to Town; The Christmas Song; Morning Has Broken; Happy Christmas (War Is Over); White Christmas; God Rest Ye Merry Gentlemen; Jingle Bell Rock; Hark the Herald Angels Sing; Silver Bells; You Make It Feel Like Christmas; O Holy Night
Album peak: No. 8
Noteworthy: Diamond offered one original, You Make It Feel Like Christmas, which he'd first recorded on *Primitive*.

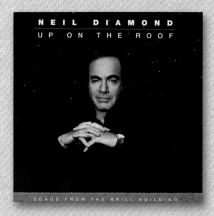

Up on the Roof: Songs from the Brill Building • 1993
Producer: Peter Asher
Label: Columbia
Songs: You've Lost That Lovin' Feelin'; Up on the Roof; Love Potion Number Nine; Will You Love Me Tomorrow; Don't Be Cruel; Do Wah Diddy Diddy; I (Who Have Nothing); Do You Know the Way to San Jose?; Don't Make Me Over; River Deep, Mountain High; A Groovy Kind of Love; Spanish Harlem; Sweets for My Sweet; Happy Birthday Sweet Sixteen; Ten Lonely Guys; Save the Last Dance for Me
Album peak: No. 28
Noteworthy: Some of these classics were duets, with Dolly Parton on You've Lost That Lovin' Feelin' and Mary's Danish on Do Wah Diddy Diddy.

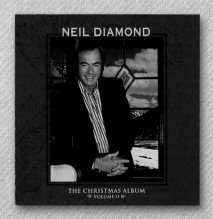

The Christmas Album, Vol. 2 • 1994
Producer: Peter Asher
Label: Columbia
Songs: Joy to the World; Mary's Little Boy Child; Deck the Halls/We Wish You a Merry Christmas; Winter Wonderland; Have Yourself a Merry Little Christmas; I'll Be Home for Christmas; Rudolph the Red-Nosed Reindeer; Sleigh Ride; Candlelight Carol; Away in a Manger; O Come All Ye Faithful; O Little Town of Bethlehem; Angels We Have Heard on High; The First Noel; Hallelujah Chorus
Album peak: No. 51
Noteworthy: Neil stepped out of the Christmas comfort zone, with a reggae arrangement on Rudolph the Red-Nosed Reindeer and a barbershop quartet–style medley of Deck the Halls and We Wish You a Merry Christmas.

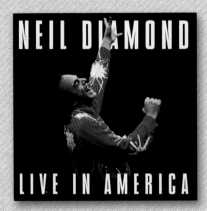

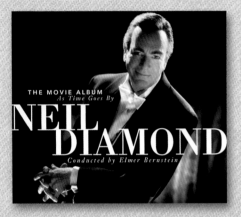

Live in America • 1994
Producer: Neil Diamond
Label: Columbia
Songs: America; Hello Again; Kentucky Woman; You Got to Me; Cherry, Cherry; I'm a Believer; Sweet Caroline; Love on the Rocks; Hooked on the Memory of You; Lady Oh; Beautiful Noise; Play Me; Up on the Roof; You've Lost that Lovin' Feelin'; River Deep, Mountain High; I (Who Have Nothing); Missa; Soolaimon; Holly Holy; And the Grass Won't Pay No Mind; You Don't Bring Me Flowers; September Morn; Havah Nagilah; Solitary Man; Red, Red Wine; Song Sung Blue; Forever in Blue Jeans; Heartlight; Cracklin' Rosie; I Am . . . I Said; Crunchy Granola Suite; Brother Love's Traveling Salvation Show
Album peak: No. 93
Noteworthy: His new live version of Red, Red Wine reflected the hit 1983 arrangement by England's UB40.

The Movie Album: As Time Goes By • 1998
Producer: Bob Gaudio
Label: Columbia
Songs: As Time Goes By; Secret Love; Unchained Melody; Can You Feel the Love Tonight; The Way You Look Tonight; Love with the Proper Stranger; Puttin' on the Ritz; When You Wish Upon a Star; The Windmills of Your Mind; Ebb Tide; True Love; My Heart Will Go On; The Look of Love; In the Still of the Night; Moon River; Ruby; Sinatra Suite: I've Got You Under My Skin/One for My Baby; And I Love Her; Can't Help Falling in Love; As Time Goes By (reprise)
Album peak: No. 31
Noteworthy: Elmer Bernstein conducted an eighty-piece orchestra for this album.

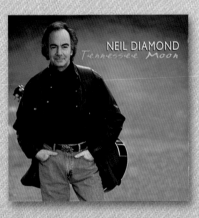

Tennessee Moon • 1996
Producers: Bob Gaudio, Richard Landis, and Paul Worley
Label: Columbia
Songs: Tennessee Moon; One Good Love; Shame; A Matter of Love; Marry Me; Deep Inside of You; Gold Don't Rust; Like You Do; Can Anybody Hear Me; Win the World; No Limit; Reminisce for a While; Kentucky Woman; If I Lost My Way; Everybody; Talking Optimist Blues (Good Day Today); Open Wide These Prison Doors; Blue Highway
Album peak: No. 14 (and No. 3 country)
Noteworthy: For this made-in-Nashville project, Diamond co-wrote with many Music City stalwarts, including Harlan Howard, Gary Burr, Dennis Morgan, and Beth Nielsen Chapman. He also co-wrote Everybody with his son, Jesse Diamond, while Waylon Jennings performed a duet with Diamond on One Good Love, and Chet Atkins appeared on Blue Highway.

Three Chord Opera • 2001
Producer: Peter Asher
Label: Columbia
Songs: I Haven't Played This Song in Years; Don't Look Down; I Believe in Happy Endings; At the Movies; Midnight Dream; You Are the Best Part of Me; Baby Let's Drive; My Special Someone; A Mission of Love; Elijah's Song; Leave a Little Room for God; Turn Down the Lights
Album peak: No. 15
Noteworthy: This was Diamond's first album of all original material written solely by Neil in—gulp—twenty-seven years.

Stages: Performances 1970–2002 • 2003
Producers: Neil Diamond and Sam Cole
Label: Columbia
Songs: Overture; America; A Mission of Love; Hello Again; Kentucky Woman; The Boat That I Row; Cherry, Cherry; Red, Red Wine; I'm a Believer; Play Me; Love on the Rocks; Soolaimon; If You Know What I Mean; Beautiful Noise; Girl, You'll Be a Woman Soon; I Haven't Played This Song in Years; You Are the Best Part of Me; Forever in Blue Jeans; Starflight; Captain Sunshine; Holly Holy; Sweet Caroline; Sweet Caroline (reprise); You Don't Bring Me Flowers; Yes I Will/Lady Magdalene; Shilo; He Ain't Heavy . . . He's My Brother; I Am . . . I Said; Cracklin' Rosie; Brother Love's Traveling Salvation Show; America (walk off); Lordy; Brooklyn Roads; Home Is a Wounded Heart; The Last Picasso; The Last Thing on My Mind; You Got To Me; God Only Knows; Lay Lady Lay; Glory Road; Rocket Man; Say Maybe; Once in a While; Rainy Day Song; Guitar Heaven; Songs of Life; Fire on the Tracks; Brooklyn on a Saturday Night; Primitive; The Story of My Life; This Time; The American Popular Song; Teach Me Tonight; Dedicated to the One I Love; Spanish Harlem; Beatles Medley: Golden Slumbers/Carry That Weight/The End; Sweet L.A. Days; Fortune of the Night; Mountains of Love; If There Were No Dreams; All I Really Need Is You; Yesterday's Songs; Can Anybody Hear Me; Talking Optimist Blues; Everybody; Marry Me; In My Lifetime; I Got the Feelin' (Oh No, No); Longfellow Serenade; Unchained Melody; I Believe in Happy Endings; O Holy Night; Silent Night; White Christmas; Rudolph the Red Nosed Reindeer; O Come, O Come Emmanuel; Little Drummer Boy; Morning Has Broken; You Make It Feel Like Christmas; The Christmas Song; Winter Wonderland; Santa Claus Is Coming to Town; We Wish You a Merry Christmas
Noteworthy: This five-CD, one-DVD boxed set includes two live discs from Las Vegas in 2002, a live Christmas CD, and two discs that compile live tracks from over the years, ranging from Lordy in 1970 to I Believe in Happy Endings in 2001.

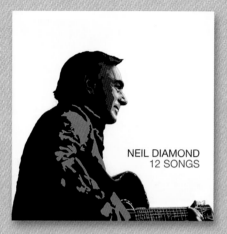

12 Songs • 2005
Producer: Rick Rubin
Label: Columbia
Songs: Oh Mary; Hell Yeah; Captain of a Shipwreck; Evermore; Save Me a Saturday Night; Delirious Love; I'm on to You; What's It Gonna Be; Man of God; Create Me; Face Me; We
Peak: No. 4
Noteworthy: After Columbia released this in a specially coded CD to prevent piracy that inadvertently became virulent to computers, the discs were recalled and a new version of the CD was issued in 2006, with the addition of Men Are So Easy and Delirious Love featuring Brian Wilson.

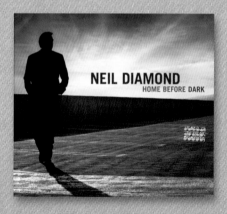

Home Before Dark • 2008
Producer: Rick Rubin
Label: Columbia
Songs: If I Don't See You Again; Pretty Amazing Grace; Don't Go There; Another Day (That Time Forgot); One More Bite of the Apple; Forgotten; Act Like a Man; Whose Hands Are These; No Words; The Power of Two; Slow It Down; Home Before Dark
Album peak: No. 1
Noteworthy: There are no drums on this disc. Natalie Maines of the Dixie Chicks performs a duet on Another Day (That Time Forgot).

Acknowledgments

Where it began: WDGY and KDWB (the latter still Minnesota's top Top 40 station) and my older brother Rick's 8-tracks of Neil (he still has 'em, along with plenty of CDs). . . . Then, there have been the many believers along the way who deserve my heartfelt thanks . . . Dave Nimmer, who hired me at the *Minneapolis Star* and dug the introspective Diamond . . . publicists who set up the interviews and the concert tickets, including the late, wonderfully eccentric Paul Wasserman, who always delivered his big-name clients, even though I didn't always have the biggest circulation; publicist extraordinaire Sherrie Levy, who always delivered Diamond and never would let me buy her dinner when she came to the Twin Cities; the expansive PR teams at Scoop and BWR, who went out of their way to accommodate my early deadlines for talking to Neil; Maureen O'Connor, Eileen Thompson, and the folks at Rogers and Cowan who treat me right at the various Grammy functions; and Heidi Ellen Robinson, who has hooked me up with countless clients, including Rick Rubin, for more than thirty-five years . . . *Los Angeles Times* critic Robert Hilburn, who understood the Diamond phenomenon and always gave his honest opinion about Neil, even if it wasn't the hip thing for a self-respecting critic to do . . . Rich Wiseman and David Wild, neither of whom I've met, for getting behind the music . . . *Boston Globe* critic Steve Morse for his friendship and feedback, hospitality and humor . . . *San Diego Union Tribune* critic George Varga for many Grammy moments and Hall of Fame good times . . . Detroit critic Gary (Mr. Phoner) Graff, who always steps up to the plate to contribute quotes from his nonstop parade of music-star interviews . . . my immediate editors at the *Minneapolis Star Tribune*, who have put up with my quirky hours and prickly opinions: Peter Vaughan, David Eden, Chris Beringer, John Habich, and Tim Campbell . . . my fellow *Strib* critic Chris Riemenschneider, who challenges and inspires me with his impersonation of my younger self . . . *Strib* managers Bob Schafer, who generously guided me through company copyright policies, and Christine Ledbetter, who consistently supports my idiosyncratic ways . . . Ken Abdo and Christie Rothenberg Healey for their sage advice . . . the folks at Voyageur Press, including editor Dennis Pernu, a persistent believer and resourceful and discriminating gatherer of photos and memorabilia; publisher Michael Dregni, who has great taste in music and great instincts about music books; publicist John Wurm, who works the U.S. mail, e-mail, and phones; Amy Glaser, for the editorial expertise, both photo- and word-related; and Krystyna Borgen for the photo research . . . Debra Senske at Getty Images for her patience and assistance . . . Cindy Shunko Jacobsma, so modest despite her talent, for graciously allowing us to share with you a few of her magnificent photographs . . . George Shuba, Cleveland's First Rock and Roll Photographer, for those fabulous early-era images, including Neil with his beard . . . Peggy Mayer for following Neil and then hanging on to all that great memorabilia over the years . . . Tom Collins for much amazing merch . . . Karin Thieme in Germany for sharing a few pieces from her collection and her fabulous art portfolio . . . Karen Iffert for (safe to say) probably the only youth hockey program in which Neil has taken out a one-page ad . . . Jeff and Bill Collins and Ralph Bukofzer for sharing the wonderful early, early singles . . . Pete Howard for the '71 Seattle concert poster . . . those special Twin Cities Diamondheads who tolerate my opinions: Marlee Ruane, Linda Schildgen, Michelle Stimpson, and Wendy Paulson . . . Martin Zellar for doing Neil! . . . B3 for endless ideas, JDK for Cambridge, M for NYC, Q for lyrics, Sa for CPA, and Hondo for magic . . . Andrew for being a masterful webmaster, an extraordinary son, and a constant inspiration who always makes me proud to be his father . . . Jan for her patience, tolerance, support, love, and muffins . . . Rex for being the best four-legged friend and leaving me a chair in which to write this book (we miss you madly) . . . Rose for being my best customer, proudest fan, and my mom . . . and last and most, Neil Diamond, for the music and the concerts, the conversations and the candor, the frog and the *mensch*.

Index

Overleaf: Back in 1978, midway through a show at Chicago Stadium, Neil would ask for the house lights to be turned on and invite the audience to stand up and join him in "Dancin' in the Streets." A fan named Chris Keckler made this banner to unfurl for Diamond to see while the house lights were up. Photographer Cindy Shunko Jacobsma recalls that Keckler was possibly in the fifteenth row (that's him behind the "IS") and that she was in the first row. "When I saw the banner roll out," Cindy explains, "I quickly stood up on my seat just long enough to point over the heads of those behind me, focus, frame, and shoot."
Cindy Shunko Jacobsma

Q: How do you want to be remembered?

A: Some people will like me and some people won't remember me. And some people will hate me and some people won't give a shit and life will go on . . . the world will continue to turn and so will our stage.

—Neil Diamond, 1986